INVEST
THEN REST

HOW TO BUY SINGLE-FAMILY
RENTAL PROPERTIES

What People Are Saying About Adiel Gorel

"It's changed my life. My wife and I have the flexibility to move around as we please. I retired ten years ago at age 53. Now I have time to volunteer with the Association of Retired Firefighters, something that's near and dear to my heart. A lot of retirees have to get second jobs to stay here in the Bay Area. I don't have to work. If we didn't have my single-family homes generating income for us, we couldn't stay here."
—*Larry S., retired fireman*

"Buying rental homes has allowed me to build my own wealth and financial independence. I've become less dependent on corporate forces. I'm very happy that I did this. I've continued to work in my industry, but I'm no longer solely dependent on a job for my income and my quality of life."
—*Michael S., healthcare industry executive*

"Investing in single-family rental homes was the best decision my husband and I made, other than getting married. Knowing that we've done so well over the years, there's no stopping us now. As we get closer to retirement age, we'll buy more rental homes for the long term."
—*Dawn D., graphic designer*

INVEST
THEN REST

HOW TO BUY SINGLE-FAMILY
RENTAL PROPERTIES

Adiel Gorel

PROGRESS PRESS
SAN RAFAEL, CALIFORNIA

Progress Press
165 North Redwood Drive, Ste #150
San Rafael, CA
94903

icgre.com
info@icgre.com

Ordering Information:
Quantity sales. Special discounts are available on quantity purchases by corporations, associations, and others. For details, contact the "Special Sales Department" at the address above.

Names: Gorel, Adiel, author.
Title: Invest then rest : how to buy single-family rental propoerties / Adiel Gorel.
Description: Includes index. | San Rafael, CA: Progress Press, 2022.
Identifiers: LCCN: 2021925471 | ISBN: 978-1-7324494-8-0 (paperback) | 978-1-7324494-9-7 (ebook)
Subjects: LCSH Real estate investment--United States. | Retirement--Planning. | Retirement income--United States. | Real property. | Finance, Personal. | BISAC BUSINESS & ECONOMICS / Real Estate.
Classification: LCC HD1379 .G67 2022 | DDC 332.6/324--dc23

*This book is dedicated to our market teams,
thanks to whom we have the solid infrastructure
enabling us to invest in the best markets.*

ACKNOWLEDGMENTS

This book was created to give investors the 30,000-foot view of the simple process of buying quality single-family rental homes, financing them with 30-year fixed-rate loans, which never keep up with inflation, and using local property managers in the most appropriate metropolitan areas in the U.S., buying in affordable markets—regardless of where the owner lives.

As part of this message, this book includes investors' stories in their own words. My deep gratitude is extended to the investors who were generous and shared their personal stories for the enrichment of the readers of this book.

Special thanks to Graciela Tiscareño-Sato, an accomplished writer and published author in her own right, for taking the time to interview the investors, get to know them and their stories, and helping me include them in this book. Graciela, thank you so much for contributing and helping make this book a reality.

Thanks to the tireless property managers, brokers, and all of our infrastructure teams in the Sun Belt Metropolitan areas in which we currently invest. Thank you for supporting me and our investors and friends, helping everyone change their financial lives for the better, without requiring them to change their busy lifestyle, since you are handling these investment homes for them (and me).

Thanks to Meir Stein and Tsah Itic for going over the book and sharing your feedback with me. It helped me make it better.

Thanks to Paul Pavlovich for the delightful artwork for this book and the other materials created to support our investors and raise money for public television.

Thanks to Ruth Schwartz, who as my book editor and design project manager patiently got me through the rounds of revisions on this book as well as a second book and all of the public television package materials, helping me keep track and meet our deadlines.

Thanks to Ellyne Lonergan, the amazing producer of our Public Television special. This TV show, which communicated the message of this book, was viewed by many who would have otherwise not been exposed to it.

Thanks to Erin Saxton, Chad LeFevre, Jerry Adams, as well as Camper Bull, Canon Wing, Aly Castle and Lorraine Evans, for widening the platform, making our message reach more people, helping them change their futures.

And last but not least, special thanks to my children, Daphne and Daniel. You are a constant source of inspiration. I keep learning from you, and I appreciate that you also tolerate your often-busy dad. I love you!

Design: Paul Pavlovich
Photos courtesy of Shutterstock.com

CONTENTS

INTRODUCTION

It's becoming abundantly clear to more people each day: You need an investment plan because you sense you might outlive your money. It's a very real concern among today's financial planners.

Why? In October 2021, we've learned the average American savings rate is 7.3% annually[1] when the common recommendation is to save between 10% and 20% of your income.

Depending on your income, and on when you start, saving 7.3% of the money you earn may get you a somewhat decent nest egg for your future. However, in many cases, it will not be enough to provide for a worry-free, lifelong retirement.

In this book, I will support these three key messages with tips, best practices, and investor success stories compiled from my 30+ years of experience as an investor and educator.

Message #1: You can buy single-family rental homes and if you do, it can change your life.

Message #2: This is doable and, yes, easy. We have the infrastructure in place to hold your hand through the process. We've helped thousands of busy people do this.

Message #3: Go ahead, break the ice. Plan on buying a single-family rental home in the next six months. Resist analysis paralysis and overcome hesitation with action. We will be with you. You won't be alone.

It is my sincere hope that you'll take the advice in this book. My mission is to change people's lives for the better. You too can join the club of busy people, with little to no real estate experience, who created a strong, long-term financial portfolio owning multiple single-family home rentals that keep up with inflation.

The experience I bring as an investor, mentor, and educator to help you acquire single-family homes across the U.S. is unique. The tips and steps I've compiled in this book, coupled with investor stories—real people who have utilized the ecosystem I've built—will convince you that you too can do this. In these pages, I'm giving you all the information you need to take action.

Since the publication of my first book in 2001 (*Remote Controlled Real Estate Riches*), three important things have changed:

1. I've helped thousands more busy people buy single-family homes as rentals to create their investment portfolios for their future financial comfort. From couples in their mid-thirties and forties, to the middle-aged woman who realized her future social security check will barely cover basic living expenses, to couples in their sixties thinking about retirement, and even people who started investing in their seventies—I've helped many busy people craft portfolios of single-family homes to meet their long-term financial needs. I'll share some of their success stories in this book.

2. Twenty years after the publication of my first book, there's been an explosion of people taking advantage of the American tendency to not act until you feel perfectly ready to do so. There's an infinite amount of noise, conflicting info, and shady offers on the Internet that tend to cause potential investors to suffer analysis paralysis. I've seen too many people spending tons of money buying educational courses about real estate investing who never actually invest. I've seen people spend $10,000 and more for a real estate "boot camp" and still

not feel ready to buy a rental home. Sometimes these people then spend more cash on yet another course and then another. Instead of suffering analysis paralysis, they could've taken that same money, read this book full of specific tips and steps, been supported by our established infrastructure, and as a result, enjoying the benefits of their single-family home rental.

3. Lastly, in my first book, I attempted to empower potential investors, teaching them how to invest on their own, including how to build a team of brokers, realtors, property managers, and title company professionals. I've now realized that many potential investors might not want to learn to do all this themselves, especially if they're busy people. I've learned that what investors usually want and need is to have their hand held through the process of buying their first single-family home rental.

So that's the purpose of this book. I will focus on teaching you *exactly* what you need to know to start. I've built an entire ecosystem of industry professionals, so you don't have to do that other stuff.

Toward the end of each chapter, you'll see an *Ecosystem Benefit* section. Here I'll provide examples of how this infrastructure will make your experiences as an investor simpler and smoother. The professionals in the infrastructure I've built will support you as you journey into the world of investing in single-family homes to secure your financial future.

I'm an investor who's spent his career, besides investing heavily myself, helping and teaching others how and where to invest in single-family rentals. Even the iconic investor Warren Buffett, who's not typically known as an investor in homes, wanted to buy single-family rentals in the aftermath of the recession in 2012. He and I communicated back and forth on this topic, and he told me how he would prefer to buy houses. You'll read more about that conversation later in the book.

I've helped investors change their lives...and I learned that most of them did not want to go through the process alone. As a matter of fact, some who did go at it alone later wished they had made a different choice. You'll see examples of that in this book too.

In these pages, I will share only the essential information you need to know so you can stop analyzing (or perhaps over-analyzing), and as Nike® says, "JUST DO IT.®"

There is material appearing in this book, which is similar, in some cases even identical to some material in my other book, *Remote Control Retirement Riches*. That is because some material is crucial to the understanding of how to build a powerful financial future using single-family home rental investments. That essential material has to appear in this book as well, as it contains the foundational concepts that need to be conveyed so that this book is as helpful to you as possible.

To help you truly appreciate the impact my advice—and your action—can have on your future, I've included investor stories in each chapter. Reading the words of investors who jumped into action years ago will leave you motivated and eager to take the first step toward a wonderful and comfortable life like they now enjoy.

When you finish reading, you'll know enough to work with our in-place ecosystem so you can buy a rental home within about six months. Ready to get started? Let's go!

1 bea.gov/data/income-saving/personal-saving-rate

CHAPTER 1

Three Reasons You Should Invest in Single-Family Home Rentals

I've helped thousands of people buy about 10,000 single-family homes in dozens of markets across the U.S. I'm interested in teaching you how to invest in this type of asset because other assets usually aren't as powerful in the long-term. In the 30-plus years of doing this work, I've learned things about human nature, including how people think about money and future time frames. That insight motivates me to teach many people how to take specific actions that could dramatically impact their future quality of life.

First, I want to pair a few important points from my first book, *Remote Controlled Real Estate Riches*, with a peek into a possible 21st century future. It will set the stage before I make my case for these three reasons: you should invest in single-family home rentals as part of your financial plan:

- Our ever-increasing life expectancy might mean that you're likely going to outlive whatever money you've planned on having.

- The Social Security system wasn't designed to support millions of retirees who live to be 100 years old or more.

- Unless you invest to outrun inflation, it'll whittle away the buying power of your retirement funds.

In the Introduction, I listed several important developments that have taken place since the publication of my first book. I want to add scientific and technology developments to that list.

Since I wrote my first book, scientists have decoded the human genome. There already exists a genetic editor known by the acronym CRISPR (stands for Clustered Regularly Interspaced Short Palindromic Repeats) that enables scientists to change or delete undesirable genes. It's very likely that such technology will be widely available in the near future, potentially increasing lifespans dramatically.

In fact, futurist and inventor Ray Kurzweil has predicted that if you hold on for another 10 years or so, your life expectancy will be of an indeterminate length. In an article from the *The Science Explorer*, Kurzweil stated, "I believe we will reach a point around 2029 when medical technologies will add one additional year, every year, to your life expectancy."[1]

So far, technological development has consistently followed Moore's law—meaning the computational power and speed of known technologies is approximately doubling every 18 months. In the past few decades, more advances were discovered, invented, and developed than in all of human history before that. This exponential pace is visible in medicine, biotechnology, nanotechnology, and many other fields.

In one particularly fascinating development, nanotech is being developed to spray nano robots directly into your mouth. These could be preprogrammed to clean up and repair your cells. Imagine what might become possible: you're 87 years old biologically but your body (at the cellular level) has been reset to some much younger age, perhaps age 50? Age 40? Maybe even 30? If you are like me and find this research completely fascinating, I have included an article from *Smithsonian Magazine* in the endnotes as a starting point.[2]

All this (coupled with the fact that Americans are already living longer) points to a new way of thinking about life expectancy.

To really understand, let's take a step back.

In 1970, the average life expectancy was 60 to 65. In fact, the entire Social Security system was based upon this life span. It meant that benefits would be paid out to only some individuals, and then only for a few years.

Today's average life expectancy is closer to 80. And who knows what the next 20 years will bring. Healthier lifestyles, medical advances, biotechnology, nanotechnology, and genetic sciences could push the average life expectancy up to 100 years or even more. The possibility is best summed up in a future-facing campaign spotted on the U.C. Berkeley campus in spring of 2018. The banner reads "Remember when...living to 120 sounded crazy?"

So that's where I believe we might be heading. This is an enormously important thing to consider, and it is also the first reason why you should invest in single-family homes: **you may live a very long time after retirement**, and you'll need an investment plan so you can enjoy that longer life.

The empty channel and a plan to fill it

Each of us lives in two channels: one where we work, live, earn, and spend, and another where we build for the future with savings and investments. For many, the second channel is nearly empty. It's not surprising: most of us weren't taught much, if anything, about investing. Words like "financial goals" and "retirement plan" seem to belong to Wall Street experts, not to regular people like us. But in today's world, heading toward the future I've described, these are important words with which you need to become familiar. The sooner you begin, the better off you'll be. I discuss this in my other book as well. This is important.

In 1981, I came to the U.S. to finish my graduate studies in electrical engineering at Stanford University. I was your typical poor student, here on a scholarship. When I finished graduate school, I was hired by nearby Hewlett-Packard Laboratories.

Two things happened when I got my first job. First, I felt rich all of a sudden, because there was a big difference between my scholarship stipend and a Silicon Valley engineer's salary. Second, I noticed that almost without exception, many of my colleagues (who had been working for 15 to 25 years or more) didn't have much to show for those long years of work. Although they were well paid, they didn't have much in terms of financial net worth. Typically, they owned a home, two cars and a 401(k). Between their salary and their credit, they could have been financially independent after 15 or 20 years. So why weren't they? Because nobody had shown them it was even possible. They hadn't thought about the future; they hadn't created a financial plan of their own.

Regardless of your specific goals, one aspect of financial planning is the same for all of us—retirement planning. Even if retirement seems a long way off, there will come a time when you no longer wish to—or can't—work anymore.

So, I'm here to tell you financial planning is important. Without it, you might end up in a place you don't want to be: 65, retired, and living on a constantly eroding, fixed income. I want you to ensure that second channel, the one that provides for you in the future, does not remain empty.

Retirement then and now

Early in my first book, I detailed how retirement was in years past and compared it to what it had become at the time of publication in 2001. Here, I'll simply emphasize that you absolutely need to develop a financial plan for yourself because chances are there will be no pension for you. Additionally, today's seniors are finding that after funding the Social Security system for decades, the checks they looked forward to receiving barely cover their bare bones basics. There's a very good chance that what worked for our parents and grandparents isn't going to work for us. **The diminishing effectiveness of the Social Security system to provide for retirees' needs is the second reason why you should invest in single-family home rentals.**

Case in point: currently, Social Security provides a maximum of $3113 per month if one retires at the full retirement age—and that's only if you contributed the maximum amount during your lifetime. Could you live comfortably on $3113 per month? Will you even receive that maximum? What if you have to live on 75% of that amount?

Can you imagine living in that extended-life future I've described, retiring at 65 as many plan to do? What if you're alive at age 101, feeling like you're 55 or 60 and excited to keep playing tennis? Now imagine that scenario, but *without* the financial resources to enjoy your extended life. That scenario will very likely play out for many people in the next few decades.

If you're now thinking, "I'm going to need a lot of money," you're right. Not only will it have to be a lot, it will have to be inflation-proof.

A collection of building blocks composed of single-family home rentals could provide the inflation-proof, comfortable lifestyle you'd like to believe is possible.

You'll need assets that keep up with inflation

This is a book about taking charge of your future; about doing something powerful with your money that can mean the difference between living the life of your dreams and retirement poverty. I've compiled these top tips for you to learn the powerful benefits of a very specific type of financial planning—the purchase of single-family home rentals. You'll soon know enough to take action for yourself and meet your financial needs. **The inflation-beating characteristics of this type of investing comprise the third reason to add single-family homes to your plan.**

For over three decades, I've helped thousands of people buy single-family homes to use as rentals in many cities across the U.S. I'm teaching how to invest in *this* type of real estate asset because other investment types just aren't as powerful in the long-term. Let's face it—preparing for retirement is much more complicated in the 21st century. Why?

One reason involves the "corporate ladder," a concept familiar to many people. Your parents and grandparents likely experienced a single ladder (maybe two if they were really ahead of their time). They were able to retire after working for twenty or thirty years with one organization. Contrast that with the "corporate ladder" of today, which looks more like the children's game *Chutes and Ladders*. Many people climb multiple ladders, sometimes moving upward, other times making lateral moves, and even taking steps down (either self-imposed or forced there after a merger or downsizing) to hopefully move up again in the future.

Additionally, 401(k) retirement plans have replaced many company pension plans. While a 401(k) has the benefit of moving with you when you change jobs, it also means half the contributions come from your paycheck. The ever-increasing number of freelancers, entrepreneurs, and consultants who don't have the advantage of an employer's contribution means more Americans now rely solely on their own contributions to a government-sponsored retirement plan.

If you start contributing to a 401(k) or Keogh plan in your twenties or early thirties, you can theoretically amass enough wealth to be fairly comfortable when you retire. But no matter how much you put aside, inflation can wreak havoc with your nest egg and your future buying power.

In my first book, I showed how an inflation rate of 3% cuts your salary by nearly one third in a decade. I reminded readers that the costs of education, housing and healthcare had risen *much* more than the average rate of inflation. When all goods and services are factored in, one might argue that the true inflation rate is possibly 4%—or even more. And that's before your savings and purchasing power are hit by taxes. In 2021, we are seeing inflation surging even higher, and economists predict it will stay higher for years.

CONSUMER PRICES 1960–2020

	1960	1980	2000	2020
Good Loaf of Bread	0.29	0.79	1.59	3.47
Gas (1 gal.) in CA	0.31	0.95	1.95	3.50
Postage stamp	0.04	0.15	0.33	0.55
Movie Tickets	2.00	4.00	8.00	14.00

As you can see in this consumer prices chart, we're now paying at least twice as much for bread, gasoline, and movie tickets as we did 20 years ago. If prices continue to increase at this pace, it's likely that in two decades we'll be paying about twice as much for these items as we do today.

Here's the unfortunate truth: the cost of many things will go up much faster than your annual cost-of-living raise, assuming you receive one. As stated earlier, not only will you need enough money to retire comfortably, you'll need an investment program that generates inflation-proof income: income that either keeps up with or exceeds the rate of inflation. Remember, the reality of inflation virtually guarantees that during the 20 or 30 years (or more) you spend in retirement, your expenses are going to increase. Your Social Security check is very likely not going to keep pace with your expenses.

Unfortunately, most people don't even begin thinking about retirement until they're in their forties...and perhaps not even then. Regardless of your age today, let's get you thinking about it. Let's get *you* ready to take positive steps to beat inflation by buying single-family homes that also generally appreciate in value.

Historical view of inflation and real estate values

Historically, real estate values have increased at 1.5 times the rate of inflation; many individual markets have exceeded that figure. That includes waves of booms and busts. We've experienced the boom of 2004-2006 in many states, as well as the recession (as it affected real estate) of 2008-2011. Nevertheless, as of Q1 2018, the majority of U.S. markets were up to home values higher than the peak of 2006... sometimes by a lot. The COVID pandemic, which started around March 2020, created a high demand for single-family homes in the suburbs. Coupled with sharp increases in lumber prices and other building materials, and combined with extremely low interest rates, demand soared in 2020 and 2021. Supply, which was already hurting from the 2008 recession's years of few housing starts, tanked. The combination of very high demand and low supply created a boom in home prices. A market like Phoenix, for example, saw home prices shoot up over 30% in a little over a year. As of August 2021, prices in most areas are at all-time highs. There are still very few markets, usually in the Deep South, that have still not fully caught up to the 2006 peaks (but are trending up). Overall, the informal "1.5 times the rate of inflation" has held for a very long span of time, including the ups and the downs. The escalating value of your investment home, combined with a decreasing loan balance, offers the opportunity to dramatically increase your net worth with a minimum investment.

Leverage

What exactly is leverage? It's just like when you use a lever to lift something heavy. In terms of money and investments, it means you're using a small amount of money to control something worth much more.

For example, if you buy a $170,000 house with a $34,000 down payment, that's 5–1 leverage. You're using a lever of $34,000 with a loan of $136,000 to raise $170,000. (Of course, there are also loan costs and closing costs for this transaction.)

Traditionally, for many people, only real estate can easily be leveraged to such a degree. In the stock market, the highest leverage you can get is a 2–1 ratio (occasionally 3–1 on selected stocks). In other words, you may be able to buy stock for only 50% of its price, with the brokerage firm providing the other 50%. This is known as buying on margin, which is very risky. If the stock price dips below the price you paid for it, you may be forced to sell it at a loss. This is known as a "margin call."

Conceivably, you can get leverage for any investment type (i.e., if your mother offers to lend you 80% of the funds to buy stock). But when you're applying to institutions for a loan, only real estate can be leveraged 5–1 or more. In 2021, under the FNMA (Federal National Mortgage Association) guidelines, the minimum down payment allowed for an investor buying a rental home is 15%, with Private Mortgage Insurance, or PMI (no PMI is needed if you put down 20% or higher). That is a leverage of 6.67–1.

Leverage is one of the benefits of investing in real estate: you can buy a $170,000 home for as little as 20% or $34,000 down, or you can buy $1 million worth of real estate for only $200,000 down (plus loan and closing costs in both examples). It's one of the keys to building a financially secure future. There's a saying among real estate professionals: "What you owe today, you'll own tomorrow." Why? Because after your initial 20% investment, tenants pay off the remainder of the mortgage for you.

The magical 30-year fixed-rate loan

Thanks to the post-World War II strategy that enabled people to buy homes easily, we have something in this country that exists in very few places in the world, if at all: the 30-year fixed-rate loan. The fixed-rate loan is a bonanza! It's magic. It's incredible.

I was born outside the U.S., so I speak from experience when I say that if you come from another country and see what's available here, certain things stand out. A 30-year fixed-rate mortgage is one of them. Americans may take it for granted, but foreigners certainly don't.

To appreciate the miracle of the 30-year fixed-rate loan and understand how inflation becomes your ally instead of eroding assets like cash savings, let me share what happens when a person takes out a loan for one million in the local currency in many other countries. In 10 years, after making 120 payments, the balance might have grown from one million to close to 2 million or so, while paying down the principal! Why? Because the loan kept up with inflation. That's the way it's done in most other countries—loans are indexed to inflation.

Not only that, see what happened to the monthly payments in this example. The original monthly payment might have started at 4,000 per month; ten years later, the payment has likely grown to 9,000 per month or so. Can you imagine this?

Contrast that scenario with a 30-year fixed-rate loan for a $1 million purchase in the USA. When you (or your tenants) pay the loan for 10 years, your balance is down to around $740,000, depending on the interest rate. Not only that, but because of inflation, that $740,000 in 10 years will possibly have the buying power of what $500,000 can buy today. So, your $1 million loan effectively became closer to a $500,000 loan!

The monthly payment on a $1 million loan taken today at 4.25% (for an investor with good but not great credit) would be $3843. This payment will NEVER change, no matter what the rates of inflation may do! Twenty years from now, the buying power of $3843 may be well under half of what it is today, yet the payment *will not increase*. Inflation keeps eroding both the payment and the remaining mortgage balance, since they are fixed and never keep up with the cost of living.

Are you starting to see why the 30-year fixed-rate loan available to you in the U.S. is so amazing? I'll dive much deeper into this important concept in the next chapter.

Real estate values

When you buy a $170,000 property with only 20% down, and you finance the $136,000 balance with a 30-year, fixed-rate loan, you've done something very powerful for your future.

Why? Because over the long-term—which I define as a minimum of five years, and preferably ten or more—hard assets, such as real estate, will on average rise in value with the cost of living.

For example, let's say you bought a $170,000 home in an average market, where the property values don't really go up, but just keep pace with inflation. This is called "zero appreciation," although the value of the home is in fact increasing 3% per year because of inflation (when the annual inflation rate is 3%). So, after one year, your \$170,000 home will be worth \$175,100. When you put only \$34,000 down, that \$5100 value increase is a 15% return on your initial investment. This will actually be somewhat lower due to closing costs, but you get the idea.

You think that's an imaginary figure? Not at all! Consider that overall home values appreciate at 1.5 times the rate of inflation. In this case, that bumps the zero appreciation \$5100 profit up to \$7650 after one year. This translates to a 22.5% return on your \$34,000 investment after owning the rental home for just one year! Good real estate markets consistently surpass the average. (Of course, should you choose to sell the property at that point, there will be selling expenses...so why not hold on to it?)

I began investing in Las Vegas in the mid-1980s. From 1987, when I stopped buying there, to only three years later in 1990, that market had risen relatively rapidly, resulting in a few hundred percent return on my investments. Back then, minimum investor down payment requirements were only 10% (with PMI) and sometimes even 5%, which I chose to put down in Las Vegas.

Whether you make a 15% return in one year or a couple hundred percent return in three years, investing in real estate and holding it for the long term will enable your money to grow at a rate that will consistently outstrip inflation. But that isn't the only benefit. There's more good news to come.

What about the stock market?

Personally, I have nothing against the stock market. Done wisely, it's a good way to invest, and a well-rounded investment portfolio will include, at the very least, some index funds. Over the long term, the stock market also keeps up with or outstrips inflation. But real estate is by its very nature a more stable investment.

One difference (as outlined above) between investing in stocks and real estate is the opportunity to use 6–1 leverage when buying property. If you buy \$40,000 worth of stock without buying on margin

(most people don't buy on margin, because it's dangerous and badly financed), and it goes up 3%, you make $1200. If you buy a $170,000 home with $40,000 down, and it goes up 3%, you make $5100, minus transaction costs. This leverage will work against you if property values go down, but the premise of this book is that you hold your single-family home investments for the long term.

It's worth repeating: In the long term, single-family home values have risen an average of 1.5 times the rate of inflation, including the boom of 2004-2006 and the recession of 2008-2011, as well as the current 2020-2021 boom.

In addition to the drawbacks expressed above, a person who doesn't begin planning for retirement until their forties and invests mostly in stocks has lost much of the power of time and compounded interest. These benefits are frequently touted by many financial advisors as being advantageous when growing a portfolio of securities investments through decades of stock market ups and downs. Those benefits are simply less available to the person who is starting their planning closer to retirement age and choosing securities as the primary investment.

And what happens if, close to your planned retirement, the Dow Jones Industrial Average and NASDAQ suddenly have back-to-back years of 10-20% losses? Not only is your retirement money not

keeping up with inflation, it's actually disappearing—you've lost value as the underlying securities prices dropped. You must wait for your retirement nest egg to recover, if it recovers, before your retirement can begin as planned.

Of course, the same thing can happen to your real estate holdings. However, you can diversify your rental homes across markets and even regions of the country. Not all geographic locations are impacted equally by booms and busts. For example, during the recession of 2008-2011, industry sources reported that the Phoenix Metro area values dropped an average of 65%–70%. In the same period, the Oklahoma City Metro market saw only a 5% decline in home values. Such market diversification will soften the overall effect during economic downturns.

In addition, as opposed to margin calls on stocks, even if home values drop, as long as you keep making the payments on the mortgage, there will not be a "margin call" by the bank, no matter what the home value is. Additionally, during downturns, the rental market actually becomes stronger, since many would-be-buyers fear the shaky economy and stay put as renters. Owners who have sold or walked away from homes become new tenants. Thus, even during a recession, holding on to your rental home investments, making the mortgage payments, and enjoying strong rents in a strong rental market enables you to weather the storm. Your tenants continue to pay down the mortgage and you'll likely come out well on the other side.

The biggest risk you can take with your money is not investing it at all. So, while there are advantages to investing in the stock market, I'm a believer in stability that historically outpaces inflation.

Close your eyes and think on this: What if, in 15 years, you owned ten houses in your hometown free and clear? Let's say they're average homes, by today's prices—each worth $170,000. That means you'd have an estate worth $1.7 million (in today's dollars—the number in 15 years is likely to be a lot higher). And that estate would be generating $100,000 in inflation-proof income every year.

Can you imagine how this would change your financial picture? There's one caveat: your hometown might not be the best place to purchase your ten single-family home rentals. So instead of owning ten houses in your hometown, you'll own ten houses in the best markets in the U.S.

"Impossible," you say?

But it isn't. It's much easier than you might think. Keep reading, and I'll show you how.

One Is not enough: Create a portfolio of building blocks—single-family home rentals

Does buying seven houses seem like a far-fetched notion? If you think it is, you're in the majority. Most of us are raised with a singular goal: to buy our own home. The home you own and live in is probably your biggest asset, yet most of us don't think beyond our first home purchase, unless it's to trade up to a larger, more expensive house.

I remember being in New York in the year 2000, on my way to give a lecture. The cab driver, a friendly fellow in his fifties, asked what I would be lecturing on. When I said real estate, he told me about his house in upstate New York. He'd bought it for only $20,000. Twenty-five years later, it was worth over $525,000...in 2000. He was proud of his investment, for good reason. But I couldn't help thinking what I always think when I hear stories like this (and I hear many): Why didn't he buy two houses? Or three? He could've maybe been a millionaire that year and wouldn't have had to drive a cab!

I understand that buying even one investment home requires a kind of quantum jump in the way you think about yourself and your future. But to buy 7, or 10, or 15 homes? Only the most experienced investors would do that, right?

Wrong.

Ask any one of the thousands of busy people whom I've worked with over the past 35 years. None of them are experts, and yet many of them have purchased 5, 10, 15, or 20 homes or more. The only possible difference between you and them is that their financial future is secure. It's a done deal. They don't have to worry about it anymore.

RETIREMENT INCOME from RENTAL PROPERTY				
	Total Income (mo.)	Total Expense (mo.)	Total Profit (mo.)	Total Profit (annual)
1 Rental Property	$1,400	$550	$850	$10,200
2 Rental Property	$2,800	$1,100	$1,700	$20,400
3 Rental Property	$4,200	$1,650	$2,550	$30,600
4 Rental Property	$5,600	$2,200	$3,400	$40,800
5 Rental Property	$7,000	$2,750	$4,250	$51,000
6 Rental Property	$8,400	$3,300	$5,100	$61,200
7 Rental Property	$9,800	$3,850	$5,950	$71,400

When studying this chart, you might have this thought that we're playing Monopoly®. And in a way we are: creating real, inflation-proof wealth by investing in multiple single-family homes (but we're never buying hotels). And you can do it just like the thousands of people I've helped already.

You can buy single-family homes where it makes sense to buy

When buying single-family rental homes, you aren't limited to where you live. You can invest in homes where prices are affordable, and rents are high relative to payment *regardless of where you happen to live.*

For example, when I began my investing, I lived in Palo Alto, California, home of Stanford University. Did that mean I was doomed to only buy single-family homes in pricey Palo Alto?

No, of course not.

In 2021, there are several cities (throughout the San Francisco Bay area and across the country) with a median home price of over $1,000,000. If you're reading this book and live in a place where houses are expensive, the notion of buying more than one home may feel even scarier.

However, when you buy seven homes for $170,000 each, the total value of all seven homes would be $1,190,000, about the same as, or less than, the median price for one home in San Francisco. When you think about it in those terms, buying seven homes may not sound very daunting at all.

Geography needn't be a limiting factor when you're building your portfolio of single-family homes. I've helped clients on the East Coast invest in the southwestern U.S.; I've helped clients on the West Coast invest in new homes being built in Florida and Oklahoma. The important message for you is to not limit yourself to thinking you should only invest in cities close to where you live.

You may be fortunate and coincidentally be living in one of the Sun Belt states where we love to invest. Regardless of your zip code, you can invest in single-family homes being built in El Paso or in Phoenix (where the prices are already too high relative to rents as of 2021) or even Baton Rouge. Thousands of people have invested in single-family homes far from where they happen to live—it's a huge country with opportunities in many markets. That's why my company keeps an eye on the most interesting developments in dynamic markets that meet the criteria I'll detail for you in Chapter 4.

ECOSYSTEM BENEFIT
Trust and the Power of Numbers

Throughout this book, I'll include the words of actual ICG investors who have purchased single-family homes. I want you to hear directly from them about their experiences utilizing the infrastructure I've built through the years. I hope you find their words instructive and inspirational.

> "In the beginning, new to the world of buying single-family home rentals, I felt a bit intimidated by the process. Because of Adiel's network, especially the brokers and title companies, I realized it wasn't such a daunting process. My trust in his

system made me comfortable. That trust is critical. All the industry people working with Adiel have your best interest at heart. I always know I can trust him and the people he chooses to bring into the ICG infrastructure. I can trust them because they depend on him and his clients. The power of large numbers works well for each of us little investors. This is why you can really trust your property managers.

"For example, when I bought two properties in one area, I initially encountered a terrible property management company. They were disorganized, there was no go-to person there. I complained to Adiel, who shared he was hearing similar stories from other investors. He got another property management company lined up for us. I've been very happy ever since. Would I have gotten that same result if I was trying to solve this problem for myself?" —*Brad H., an employee at a hospital and ICG investor since 1991; Brad owns 10 single-family homes in Phoenix, two in San Antonio, and two in Oklahoma City.*

INVESTOR STORY
In His Own Words

Jack was working for an environmental consulting company and said he began buying single-family homes because he had a "basic awareness and had been influenced by my parents who owned rental properties."

Jack had read Bill Nickerson's book in the 1970s titled, *How I Turned $1000 into a Million in Real Estate in My Spare Time.* Jack participated in a monthly real estate educational group in San Francisco. They invited expert speakers to come and present in an effort to learn together and get different viewpoints.

"Adiel was one of our speakers," shared Jack. "His approach made a lot of sense. I liked that there was group support and

shared knowledge, but ultimately it was *my* investment to make, rent, keep, and enjoy. I have support from the group if I need it, when I buy, sell or want to learn something new."

I asked how following this advice has changed his life. Jack said this: "I own several units in the Bay Area and after having sold a few of my properties in Arizona, I own over a dozen homes in the greater Phoenix area. I once sold a home in the San Francisco East Bay and immediately bought three homes in Arizona. This portfolio is my major source of income now. I wouldn't have this lifestyle and income if I hadn't done this. I'd probably still be working. I had a full-time job when I started investing in rental homes. I retired ten years ago. I have the luxury of managing my properties here inthe Bay Area while also hiring property managersfor my out-of-state investments. Those remote property managers make it effortless."

— Jack, ICG investor since the 1990s (who began investing in the 1980s in his early forties); today he owns several units in the Bay Area and over a dozen rental homes in the greater Phoenix area.

REPLAY

- Everyone needs to plan for retirement.
- You can't count on Social Security benefits alone.
- People are retiring earlier and living longer. You may need enough money in retirement to live on for 20, 30, or even 40 years—and with genetics, medicine, and bio-tech advances, possibly much longer.
- 3% inflation decreases your purchasing power by one-third in only 10 years.
- You'll need assets that keep up with inflation.
- Use the magical 30-year fixed-rate loan and inflation becomes your ally.
- Assets that keep up with inflation and a loan that doesn't make for a sweet combination.
- The biggest risk you take with your money is not investing it.
- Leverage offers the ability to dramatically increase your net worth with a minimum investment.
- A 30-year fixed-rate loan actually makes money for you.
- Real estate overall has historically appreciated at about 1.5 times the rate of inflation over the long term, even taking into account occasional booms and busts.
- Use real estate as an inflation-proof investment for financial goals, and as an inflation-proof income for retirement.
- Think beyond your first purchase: 5, 10 and even 20 homes are likely within your reach, especially in less expensive markets.

---

1 thescienceexplorer.com/brain-and-body/google-s-leading-futurist-predicts-humans-will-start-living-forever-2029

2 smithsonianmag.com/smart-news/scientists-test-out-tiny-robots-meant-travel-inside-human-body-180953937

CHAPTER 2

Use a 30-Year Fixed-Rate Loan with 20% Down Payment to Buy Your Rental Homes

In my first book, I dedicated an entire chapter to financing. I mentioned different types of loans available for investing in single-family homes and stated there are only three types of loans I recommend you use. You're welcome to read up on those options. However, based on the reasons I hinted at in the first chapter (and other reasons you'll soon see) here's the best-practice tip I want to share with you in this chapter: wherever possible, use the 30-year fixed-rate loan with a 20% down payment to build your portfolio of single-family homes.

A fixed-rate mortgage simply means the interest rate on the loan will not change and you'll know exactly what your monthly payments will be for the entire loan term. A 30-year loan offers the most flexibility; you can think of it as containing the 15-year loan, the 18-year loan, or even the 10-year loan. If you choose, you can make extra payments on the loan principal and pay off the loan years sooner to fit your financial plan (but you aren't required to do so). I'll show you numerical examples in this chapter.

I find the 30-year loan superior to the 15-year loan because scheduled monthly payments are smaller for the former (in good times, you can always pay more, but in lean times, you cannot pay less). A smaller payment frees up more of your income for other purposes. This enables you to fund retirement accounts or save your cash to buy additional rental homes.

Fixed-rate loans generally carry a slightly higher interest rate than adjustable or short-term loans because the lender is making a commitment to lend money at a fixed-rate over a longer term. Remember, inflation will effectively reduce the cost of your monthly payment obligation year after year. A fixed-rate loan with a payment that doesn't change over the life of your investment provides you with a monthly payment whose present value will erode over time.

It's likely obvious that you'll want the lowest interest rate possible, yet not everyone will qualify for the lowest interest rate available. The rate you'll be offered will depend upon your credit worthiness and other factors. If the interest rate for fixed-rate loans is high (well above the Q2 2021 investors' rate of about 3.8%) or if the only fixed-rate loan for which you qualify is two or three points above the best rate, then perhaps you'll want to consider other financing options: an adjustable-rate mortgage (ARM) or a hybrid mortgage.

There's a mountain of information available elsewhere if you're curious about ARMs or hybrid loans. But in this chapter, I will only focus on the recommended loan type for investing in single-family homes: the 30-year fixed-rate loan. My goal is to share what you need to know to buy a single-family home rental soon.

 **PAUSE**

In this book, I'll be talking about 30-year, fixed-rate loans. It's important to keep one thing in mind: you don't have to take 30 years to pay off a 30-year loan. You can pay it off whenever you want to—whatever works for your particular financial plan. You can also refinance the original loan to a 15-year note or make additional principal payments to reduce the time it takes to own the rental home free and clear. Some advantages of a 30-year loan are its smaller monthly payments, the fact that inflation has a longer time to erode its real value with the years, and that it's typically easier to qualify for a longer term/ smaller payment. As your investment home value increases and rental prices rise, you can decide whether to keep the profits or use them to pay off the loan sooner.

The miracle of the American fixed-rate loan — revisited

As an investor, your safest course is to go with a 30-year fixed- rate loan. This keeps your payments stable over the life of your investment, which helps you to estimate cash flow, expenses, profits, taxes, and so on. My main reason for recommending it is this: the cost of the loan actually erodes as the cost-of-living rises. Don't be afraid of the 30-year term. You can pay the loan off at any time—after 5, 11 or 16 years—usually without paying a penalty. Thirty-year, fixed-rate financing is the ultimate no-brainer. Once you have it in place, you don't have to think about it again.

Let's take a look at the numbers: When you take out a $136,000 30-year loan, say at a 5% fixed-rate (I am using a high interest rate on purpose. As of Q2 2021, investor rates are about 3.8%. However, over the decades I have seen rates as high as 14% and very commonly, 7% or 8% rates for many years. Inflation is starting to rear its ugly head, and it's likely rates will rise in the future. Thus, I'm using a rate of 5%, which, as of Q2 2021, is "high," but over history is considered a good low rate). Your monthly payment of principal and interest is approximately $730 a month. You know for a fact this is going to be the payment for the next 30 years—it will never change. Even in 20 years, if $730 is barely enough to buy dinner for two, it'll still be your mortgage payment.

When I speak in Europe, my audience invariably stops me when I tell them about fixed-rate loans in the U.S. They think I don't have my facts straight. They think it's not possible. Or they think I'm just plain crazy. They can't comprehend how, in a country where the cost-of-living keeps rising, banks will lend money for 30 years where the monthly payment

and the balance of the loan never change—except to go down. For anyone from outside the U.S., this is truly an unbelievable thing. In other countries, loans are indexed to inflation.

As outlined in the previous chapter, an initial payment of 730 a month (in the local currency) on a 136,000 loan could have ballooned 10 years later to a payment of 1500 or so a month by keeping up with local inflation! And the balance of the loan? It could have grown from 136,000 to 250,000 or so, keeping up with that same inflation (and paying down principal along the way). Why? Because normally, in most countries, both the monthly payment and the balance of the loan increase to keep up with inflation.

So, you see, fixed-rate loans are not just inflation-proof, they're *inflation fighters*.

Here in the U.S. however, you can buy single-family homes with the magical 30-year fixed-rate loan and become allies with inflation. Those of us who speak with an accent truly see the magical properties of the 30-year fixed-rate loan. We have examples of what loan balances look like when loans don't erode with, but instead keep up with, inflation. It's more difficult to build up your net worth holding loans indexed to inflation.

I want Americans to share this understanding. It's so powerful to appreciate this principle of how letting inflation erode the loan balance of your single-family home rentals purchased with 30-year fixed-rate loans can change your life in the years to come. I feel so passionately about this point that I often feel like grabbing people by the collar, saying, "Wake up! Do you understand how important this is to your future wealth and net worth?"

In my experience, though, I find that many people do not understand the **time value of money.** They have instead has been led astray thinking about interest calculations of the 30-year fixed-rate loan. It shows up when someone says, "I'm not sure I should take out a 30-year fixed loan because I'll end up paying $300,000 in interest." That's how I know someone doesn't fully understand the time value of money.

Here's my response to that: bring those future dollars you're worried about paying as interest into the **present value**. Those future interest dollars you're worried about paying are going to be worth so much *less* in today's buying power (nowhere near $300,000 in the example above!) Then you'll see what you're really paying on the loan, and it's much less than it seems.

All these big numbers of eventual interest you'll pay are meaningless because many of them are from decades into the future in an inflationary environment.

There's a so-called banker's secret that tells people to avoid paying lots of interest, so pay off your 30-year loan in 10 years or so. Frankly, I find that ridiculous because you're preventing inflation from naturally eroding the loan. And you're using your cash that you could've instead used to buy more rental homes.

I'm an engineer, so just for fun, let's take this to its logical conclusion. Want to buy a $170,000 property but aren't convinced about the miraculous power of the 30-year fixed-rate loan because you're fixated on that $300,000 in interest over three decades?

Then *don't get a loan*. Pay all cash. There, now you've paid zero interest for your single-family home investment. But because you did that, you also don't have that cash with which you could've bought additional homes. Your cash is gone because you didn't want to pay any interest. Not a win! You also missed out because you never gave inflation a chance to erode a loan over the years.

The other extreme? I said it in my first book: If they had 50-year fixed-rate loans available, I'd be the first in line to get one. All the benefits I've outlined above get even better with a 50-year horizon— once you understand the time value of money. And, of course, I can choose to pay off the 50-year loan in 30, 15, 11, 9 or any other number of years between zero and fifty.

We've already seen how the price of everything is steadily going up because of inflation. Everything goes up, except your mortgage balance, (which is also reduced every month as each principal payment is applied), and your mortgage payment, which remains static but because of inflation is actually eroding—the present value buying power of each monthly payment is getting smaller and smaller all the time, as is the case with the remaining outstanding balance of the mortgage. In fact, when you really understand this, you'll see that by financing your investment with a fixed-rate loan, you're actually making money in the long-term. Here's an analogy:

Imagine that, if in 1980 you had made a deal with Whole Foods (the year it was founded) that you would never have to pay more than 25 cents for a single organic avocado for the next thirty years; after that your organic avocados would be free. Imagine that! In 1990, when everyone else was shelling out 65 cents for an organic avocado, your deal looked pretty good. Now, when an organic avocado might cost $2.00, your deal is even better. And in 10 years, when an organic avocado is likely to cost $3.00 or more, your organic avocado will be absolutely free! Financially, you will feel fabulous having enjoyed this long-term deal with Whole Foods.

Some of the examples in this chapter also appear in my other book, as they are essential to understanding the concept.

Why I recommend you choose a 20% down payment when you buy rental homes

There are three reasons I recommend using a 20% down payment with your 30-year fixed-rate loan:

1. Get the biggest investor loan you can and let inflation erode it.

2. Preserve your cash as much as possible to prepare to buy your next single-family home.

3. Avoid the pain of paying Private Mortgage Insurance (PMI) if you choose to pay minimal required down payment (15%) as an investor.

In the 1980s when I began investing, the minimum down payment was 10% for investors to get a 30-year fixed-rate loan. Then came the recessionary downturns. Foreclosed homes were being sold by the Veterans Administration and the Department of Housing and Urban Development and investors could buy those homes with only 5% or 3%—or even $1000—down. I always put down the minimum required for two reasons:

1. I didn't have an infinite amount of cash. I wanted to use my cash powerfully and preserve as much as possible. The less I put down, the more cash I had to buy additional homes.

2. If I just finished extolling the virtues of the amazing 30-year fixed rate loan that never keeps up with inflation, why do I want to make it a smaller loan at the beginning? (Hint: I don't! I *want* it to be a bigger loan.)

The combination between preserving my hard-earned cash to use it more powerfully (buying two homes instead of one), coupled with getting the bigger, amazing loan that would erode with inflation, always made me as an aggressive, numbers-oriented investor who wanted to pay the least amount possible as a down payment for a rental home. As of 2018, Federal National Mortgage Association (Fannie Mae) guidelines allow an investor to buy with as little as 15% down payment, meaning a loan for 85% of the purchase price. Any down payment less than 20% requires private mortgage insurance (PMI), as explained below. If you use a 20% down payment, you'll avoid paying PMI.

Having said that, I'll state that on occasion I have chosen to use the minimum 15% down payment option, to preserve cash, and paid the PMI. I'll explain it briefly below, for completeness. Then you'll see why I recommend you avoid the pain of PMI and just put 20% down for your single-family home rentals.

Have you recently purchased a primary residence? Here's something to know: the interest rate you were quoted for a 30-year fixed-rate loan as a *homeowner* will very likely be lower than the rate you'll be quoted for the same type of loan when you're buying as an *investor*. That's the nature of the industry. This is another reason why I advise you tilt the scale in favor of putting 20% down: less hassle in the future and typically a slightly lower interest rate.

Private mortgage insurance: to pay or not to pay?

When using a down payment of less than 20%, lenders require that you carry private mortgage insurance (PMI). Common (mortgage industry) wisdom states that borrowers who have less than a 20% stake in their property are more likely to default. Private mortgage insurance protects lenders (not borrowers) from financial loss if the home goes into foreclosure. Typically, a portion of the PMI premium is paid at closing; a payment representing 1/12 of the annual premium is paid monthly with the loan's principal and interest.

Remember, in the previous section, when I mentioned the interest rate for a 30-year fixed-rate loan as an *investor* will be higher than the rate for a *homeowner* for the same loan? Well, guess what? The interest rate is also somewhat higher for a loan obtained with 15% down payment vs a loan with 20% down. Additionally, the cost of PMI for investment properties is higher than for owner-occupied properties.

For these reasons, some investors prefer to use a 20% down payment instead of 15% to avoid the pain of PMI altogether, which is usually also my recommendation.

Lastly, PMI, depending on the loan, drops off in the future once you have exceeded a certain equity threshold in the property, usually within a few years. This could be as soon as three to five years in a regular market. Even if it takes longer, say five years, the PMI on a $150,000 loan adds up to just a few thousand dollars spread over five years while preserving your cash. Which is why, at times, I've been aggressive enough to choose a 15% down payment plus PMI to free up my cash to get closer to buying my next property. I've sometimes even realized a positive monthly cash flow doing this. Personally, I prefer to use as much leverage as possible within reason.

Generally, when you compare the price of PMI to an extra 5% cash out of your pocket, paying the PMI wins. However, if you're older, have a lot of cash, and need more cash flow right away, use a 20% (or higher) down payment and skip the PMI.

Since I've mentioned these different potential life points, let's take a look at situations where you might want to pay off the 30-year fixed-rate loan sooner, depending on your age, your needs, and your financial plan.

Pay off the home sooner, if needed, to finance college expenses

Here's a financial planning dilemma I hear often from young couples. Let's take a look at Jenny and Tom, both in their thirties, who want to send their newborn daughter to college in 18 years. They know that today's university expenses are already incredibly expensive; they can't even begin to predict what higher education will cost in 18 years. They only know that they can't afford it now and can't imagine how they'll be able to afford it later. Perhaps Tom and Jenny understand the negative impacts of inflation on their planned savings and wonder what buying power they'll have in the future as their baby girl turns teenager and begins to ponder her university options.

A simple method: using real estate as a college fund

Many people get confused when trying to see 15 or even 20 years into the future. Even when you know exactly what you want (and most of us don't; we only know that we want to have enough to maintain our present standard of living), trying to estimate expenses, future financial goals and prepare for the unexpected is simply mind-boggling. Who really knows what the next 15 years will bring, or exactly how much money will be necessary to live comfortably in two decades? You might think you need a crystal ball—one that will calculate future earnings, taxes, and inflation, and provide a clear vision of what your life might look like then.

Happily, a crystal ball isn't required. You don't have to see 20 years into the future. You can estimate your future needs by thinking in today's dollars.

First, what's the cost of a four-year university education today? Current estimates place the combined costs of tuition, housing, and expenses for the 2020-2021 school year at an average of $108,000 or so for an in-state public school, $173,200 for an out-of-state public

school, and $220,000 for a private university. Let's use a blended $165,000 for this example.

What Tom and Jenny need is an investment that's inflation-proof, one that will increase in value along with the rising costs of a college education.

I suggest they buy a $200,000 home with $40,000 down and total cash needed, including loan and closing costs, of $48,000. They will finance the remaining $160,000 with a 30-year, fixed-rate loan. Instead of taking 30 years to pay off the 30-year loan, because they want to use their single-family home rental as a tool to finance their child's college education, I recommend they plan to pay the loan off in 18 years.

How? By making an extra payment on the principal every year. After a few years, their tenants' rent is likely to rise with the cost of living, but Tom and Jenny's mortgage payment will remain the same. The rental income will make the extra principal payment for them. After a few more years, the rents are still likely to be rising—so not only is the house making the extra principal payment, it's also paying them extra cash flow. For most of those 18 years, the house will be generating profits.

After 18 years, Tom and Jenny will own this $200,000 (in today's dollars) home free and clear. It will cover the cost of their daughter's $165,000 (in today's dollars) education. Both the home's value and the college expenses should keep up with the cost of living in a similar manner. There's plenty of extra here to sell the house or to refinance it eventually, and still come out ahead.

"And if you want to send your daughter to Harvard with a Porsche," I would add, "buy two houses."

RENTAL PROPERTY AS COLLEGE FUND					
	Year 1	Year 5	Year 10	Year 15	Year 18
Rental Income	$16,800	$19,654	$23,912	$29,092	$31,741
PI + $2,676 Extra Principal	$11,688	$11,688	$11,688	$11,688	$11,688
Tax & Insurance	$2,688*	$3,145	$3,836	$4655	$5,236
Property Mgmt	$1,344	$1,572	$1,913	$2,327	$2,539
Misc. Expenses	$1,800	$2,106	$2,371	$2,774	$3,120
Annual Profit/Loss	$-720	$1,142	$4,104	$7,648	$9,158
Property Value	$176,800	$206,831	$251,642	$306,160	$344,389
Mortgage Balance	$131,334	$110,020	$76,262	$32,395	$0
Gross Equity	$45,466	$96,811	$175,380	$273,765	$344,389

Using 5.25% fixed 30-year interest rate. PI for 30 years is $751/mo. PI to pay off in 18 years is $974/mo. So, pay an extra $223/mo. ($2,676/yr.) to pay loan off in 18 years. Using Oklahoma City Tax & insurance figures in 2020 for a $170,000 new house.

*The increase in rental income, tax & insurance, property management, misc. expenses, and property value has been calculated using a 4% annual rate. PI = Principal and Interest.

Pay off the home sooner, if needed, for a comfortable retirement and solid net worth

Now let's look at another demographic and a common financial dilemma they encounter. Let's turn to Marion and Paul, both in their fifties, who would like to retire in 15 years. They have a 401(k) and an IRA but, even so, they can see that another 15 years of contributions and compounding isn't going to provide them with the kind of wealth they'd like to have. Like most Baby Boomers, they don't envision spending their retirement camped out on the couch in front of the boob tube. They want to travel, play golf and tennis, and set up a trust fund for their kids. What can they do to ensure their retirement lifestyle will be all that they desire?

I asked this couple to estimate the annual income they'd need if they were to retire today. How much would it take for them to live the life of their dreams—now, in today's dollars?

They replied that $70,000 per year would cover all of their living expenses and financial goals as retirees: travel, trust fund, etc. What Marion and Paul needed was an income that was inflation-proof—one that would continue to generate the equivalent of $70,000 in today's dollars year after year...even 15 or 20 or 40 years from now.

Suppose that like Tom and Jenny, Marion and Paul bought a $170,000 home with $34,000 down (approximate total cash needed, including closing costs would be $41,000) and planned to pay off the 30-year fixed-rate loan in 15 years. This faster payoff timetable is completely up to Marion and Paul. Maybe they decide to pay the 30-year fixed-rate loan off in 18 years—it's totally flexible to meet their financial plan for retirement.

Once Marion and Paul own the home free and clear with no mortgage payment, there will continue to be expenses like property taxes, insurance, property management fees, possible vacancies, and home repairs. I can tell you from my decades of experience being involved in buying thousands of homes that these typical expenses are going to run approximately $550 a month.

Now, what's the monthly rent on a $170,000 home? Here are just two markets in the U.S. where a $170,000 home rents for approximately $1400 a month: Oklahoma City, Oklahoma and Baton Rouge, Louisiana. In areas like Tampa, Florida homes selling for $200,000 can rent for $1500 or $1600 per month. So, if Marion and Paul's house is renting for $1400 each month, and their expenses are $550 each month, that's an $850 profit per month. If one house brings in $850 per month, how many houses will they need to make $5833 per month (their stated target income of $70,000 annually?) They will need to own seven houses generating that same income level. In fact, seven homes will bring in $71,400 per year in this example. Please see the chart below. Use can use this to approximate the number of rental homes you'll need to generate the retirement income you desire to have once you stop working full time.

RETIREMENT INCOME from RENTAL PROPERTY				
	Total Income (mo.)	Total Expense (mo.)	Total Profit (mo.)	Total Profit (annual)
1 Rental Property	$1,400	$550	$850	$10,200
2 Rental Property	$2,800	$1,100	$1,700	$20,400
3 Rental Property	$4,200	$1,650	$2,550	$30,600
4 Rental Property	$5,600	$2,200	$3,400	$40,800
5 Rental Property	$7,000	$2,750	$4,250	$51,000
6 Rental Property	$8,400	$3,300	$5,100	$61,200
7 Rental Property	$9,800	$3,850	$5,950	$71,400

ECOSYSTEM BENEFIT
Work with a Lender with Proven Performance

When purchasing in states other than where you live, we can make your life easier by introducing you to a proven lender who can lend wherever you are buying. In addition, once you own several properties, there are additional benefits to being part of our infrastructure, as this investor explains:

> "I've refinanced as interest rates dropped. When I started investing, interest rates were between 8-11%. I refinanced to make these properties more profitable. All these loans are now at around 4% interest. I worked with a mortgage broker to refinance, consolidate loans, pay off a few and get overall lower interest rates. This has significantly improved my cash flow and saved thousands of dollars."— *Jack, ICG investor since the 1990s (who began investing in the 1980s in his early forties); today he owns several units in the Bay Area and over a dozen rental homes in the greater Phoenix area*

We can also make your life easier by introducing you to a mortgage broker whom we trust to perform and fund in a timely manner. Let me share something I've seen repeatedly in my 30+ years in this business, so you don't have to repeat the mistakes made by others. I've met many people who were ready to invest in their first single-family home who excitedly approached the lender who helped them get their mortgage for their primary residence. They were disappointed to learn that the person they had that relationship with wasn't licensed to initiate investor loans to buy rental homes in the state where they wanted to invest—and they didn't have recommendations for someone who did know this area. Oops.

There is another thing I've learned since the last recession when loans were hard to come by: I've heard too many stories of mortgage brokers who overpromised and under delivered—resulting in delays closing escrow and other headaches. Therefore, I've grown to appreciate performance—those true professionals who get loans funded in a timely manner. That's who we've brought into our infrastructure. Because we've helped so many investors and seen so many investor loans funded through these professionals, we'd be happy to make these connections for you. That's just one of the many benefits of working with an ecosystem of many investors and many industry professionals.

INVESTOR STORY
In Her Own Words

Theresa began investing in her late twenties while working as an auditor. She shared with me that, growing up, she heard an important cultural message: "For your family's security, before you have children, buy your own home."

She did—in 2005, in Arizona, while living in California. Her sister was traveling on business there and noticed that 2500 square-foot, new construction homes in Tucson sold for $200,000—significantly cheaper than where she lived in Northern California. She and her sister purchased homes next to each other in Tucson.

A few years later, after birthing her first child, she began to think about investing for her family's long-term financial security. She emphasized this: "Because I'm an accountant, I always think ahead. I'm the one thinking about and making plans for our financial future and for our kids."

Today Theresa owns a total of six properties in four states, including her home in the San Francisco Bay Area that she bought three years after buying the rental in Arizona. Now, the long-term-thinking mother of two school-aged children tells her daughter, "It's very important to work, save, and invest to let your money work for you." Theresa says this about her current portfolio:

> "I feel I still need to buy more homes to rent. It's not enough yet for me to stop working. I want to enjoy an early retirement. Yes, I am more financially secure, but now I'm thinking ahead again. I'm calculating what we'll need to fund the college educations of our children who are now ages nine and twelve."
> —*Theresa, ICG investor, began buying single-family homes to rent at the age 29; today at age 42, she owns two properties in Arizona, two in Oklahoma, one in Florida, and her home in the Bay Area.*

REPLAY

- **The American 30-year fixed-rate loan is a miraculous inflation-fighting financial tool.**

- **It's imperative to understand the time value of money to truly appreciate the relationship between present value, future value, and not get caught up in the minutiae of interest rates.**

- **Pair the 30-year fixed-rate loan with a 20% down payment to avoid the pain of PMI and enjoy favorable interest rates for investors.**

- **You can pay off a 30-year fixed-rate loan whenever you want to whatever works for your particular financial plan. You may want to do so to pay for your child's college education or to enjoy a comfortable retirement and solid net worth.**

CHAPTER 3

Buy Single-Family Homes and Keep Them for the Long-Term for Maximum Benefits

If you purchase an investment property intending to make a profit in less than five years (my definition of short-term), you're going to be at the mercy of the market. Trust me when I say the market has no mercy. Anytime you invest that way, you're taking a big risk with your money, because to be successful at it, you need both luck and timing on your side (so it's very much like gambling). Let me share two personal experiences so you can appreciate why I'm focusing this book on teaching you the best practices you need to buy single-family homes for the *long*-term.

In 1985, I started buying single-family homes in Las Vegas, Nevada. It was a depressed real estate market back then and houses cost about $40,000 each. I was very aggressive and bought 22 houses in my first year and a half. Many of my engineer friends at Hewlett-Packard were impressed by what I was doing. Soon I was leading a group of about 20 friends there. They also bought homes to rent in Las Vegas. We bought there until mid-1987 when the Vegas market went up dramatically.

We held onto those properties as long-term investments and turned our attention to another inexpensive market at the time—Portland, Oregon. Then in 1988, with California home prices just beginning to rise, I focused on a market closer to home: the city of Santa Rosa, 60 miles north of San Francisco.

I began by buying four houses there in January of that year, each priced at $110,000. I was assisted by two wonderful realtors named Roxanne and Rita. When I told them I was ready to buy my fifth house, these ladies connected me to a developer in Santa Rosa who had just finished building an entire subdivision. He had a whole street of unsold homes he needed to sell quickly. I offered to buy the entire street in mid-1988. I also asked for (and received) a discount since I was buying in bulk; the average price I paid was $99,000 per house and I rented them.

Then came the 1989 California market boom. Because prices were rising so quickly, I sold the entire street full of homes within ten months of purchasing. I sold for an average price of $142,000 per home—at a net profit of approximately $30,000 per property. My realtors were ecstatic –they collected commissions twice in less than one year for an entire street full of houses. As a matter of fact, they were so happy they petitioned the City of Santa Rosa to rename Omega Court to Gorel Court since I owned all the properties there. The city approved the change (after a public hearing was held) and I was told I had a street named after me. Today, you can still find Gorel Court in Santa Rosa where that short-term investment was successful.

Why am I telling you this story? I have three reasons:

1. To give you some background of how I've learned to value long-term investing.

2. To brag.

3. To powerfully illustrate the *difference* between short-term and long-term investing and why I choose to focus on the long-term.

I've described two types of investments I've done through the years: First, I bought homes in Las Vegas and other markets as rental properties to be held long-term. In the second, I purchased an entire street and sold it quickly. The latter sounds exciting and profitable (now that it's finished).

But let's look at the selling part of that short-term deal in Santa Rosa more carefully. When you're selling an entire street of homes, many things can be delayed: Maybe one of your buyers didn't qualify and fell out, so now you need to find another buyer. Maybe some buyers' loans got delayed. If any of those things would've happened in this case, I would be telling you a very different story.

I finished selling the homes on Gorel Court around May 1989. That same month, the California market started to slow down. If this deal in Santa Rosa had closed a few months later than it did, I would've lost a lot of money and been stuck with an entire street of homes all declining in value. I would be telling you a very sad story.

As it happened, I made a lot of money on this short-term deal, but it was nothing but luck and timing. That isn't what you want. You don't want to be relying on luck. Whenever you want to speculate and make a quick buck in real estate, you're taking a risk. You're hoping positive things will happen, but you'd better be financially prepared to hold on to the property for the long-term just in case circumstances turn against you.

The key takeaway of my Santa Rosa story is this: to profit doing short-term deals, you are relying on luck, timing, and unseen forces to all be in your favor. Instead, I'm here to teach you how to buy for the long term to increase your chances of creating a wonderful financial future for yourself and your family.

I use these examples in other books as well, as they are part of the foundational material of my message.

But what about flipping properties?

Just a few words about flipping properties since it's a popular topic. The flipping (selling a property very soon after you purchase it with the intention of making a quick profit) you hear about on TV is for those who are truly absorbed in the industry. And as I've just demonstrated with my Santa Rosa/Gorel Court story, quick profits in real estate rely too much on luck and timing to be a dependable source of income. It's not investing at all—it's gambling.

You're a busy person with a full life and many obligations; you're likely not looking to quit your job and flip properties which would totally consume your time. You didn't decide to read this book to become a property flipping professional. You're here to learn to take action to buy single-family home rentals and build your long-term portfolio. You're looking for actionable knowledge for your financial future.

In my book *Remote Control Retirement Riches*, I detailed "The Four Conditions of Flipping Properties." I'll only list them here:

1. You must buy below market value.
2. The market must keep rising.
3. You must find a buyer who will pay full price.
4. Your profits must exceed your actual costs.

If you're curious, you're welcome to read more about that in my other book or elsewhere. Here, I'll stay focused on the long-term horizon.

Now let's look at two wonderful forces that start to work for you when you buy: First, inflation continuously erodes your 30-year fixed-rate loan. Second, your loan is getting paid off slowly by your tenant as you enjoy equity growth. Both of these forces prove more powerful the more time you allow them to work for you.

Real estate shows its power in the long term

We've already described *how* inflation causes just about everything to go up in price as time passes. We've already seen how inflation erodes the value of the 30-year fixed-rate loan. The point I want to emphasize here as we distinguish between short- and long-term investments is this: to really let inflation erode your loan for you, I advise you to plan to keep your property at least ten years or longer. Give yourself the gift of time so inflation can do its thing.

Let inflation erode your loan while you sleep at night. Let inflation make your loan smaller and smaller in real buying power. Let inflation erode your loan as your tenants pay off that magical 30-year fixed-rate mortgage. Let inflation erode your loan as rents increase gradually with inflation. Let inflation erode your loan while the principal constantly goes down with the payments, a process that accelerates as time goes by. Eventually, this creates a lot of equity, and your net worth grows. Home values we've seen in the regions where we buy have historically increased, through both booms and recessions, at an average of approximately 1.5 times the rate of inflation.

For many investors, in time with inflation's erosion, the principal balance eventually looks small and inconsequential. In that case, you may choose to pay off the loan to own the property free and clear sooner or you may elect to let time and inflation erode it even further. Either way, this property you bought for the long term has become a building block toward fulfilling your financial goals.

So, let inflation erode your loan—the longer the better. Let's look at some numbers to cement this long-term perspective in your mind.

The chart below shows how single-family home rentals show their power over the long term. The figures in the chart represent an investment in a property priced at $180,000, with a 20% down payment, and the remaining $144,000 financed with a 30-year fixed-rate mortgage at 5% interest.

Line one shows rental income starting at $18,000 per year and rising 3% per year. Line two shows how principal and interest payments remain the same. Line three shows a 3% rise in tax and insurance each year (these figures are based on property tax rates for the state of Oklahoma; some states may be lower or higher). Line four shows property management fees increasing at 3% annually.

The fifth and sixth lines of the chart reveal how profits and property values become very powerful over the long term. Most importantly, the mortgage balance decreases as rental income and property value rise. I've calculated the increase in property value at 3% per year—a conservative figure for many markets.

You can see here that with an initial investment of about $40,000 more or less (20% down payment plus loan & closing costs), in 20 years this property will be generating nearly $16,000 per year in profit using that conservative 3% growth rate. It will have an approximate market value of $325,000, resulting in about quarter million dollars in gross equity.

If this home's price were to appreciate at an average rate of 4% annually (still a historically low average), the value in 20 years would be $394,402, and the gross equity would be $321,518.

At 5% annual average price appreciation, the value in 20 years would be $477,593 and the gross equity $404,709. Stop and think about that: over $400,000 in equity on an approximate initial $40,000 investment. This coupling of inflation eroding your loan as your tenants pay it with property value increases over the long term is why we buy single-family homes rentals and keep them for at least ten years.

LONG TERM INVESTMENT PROFITS					
	Year 1	Year 5	Year 10	Year 15	Year 20
Rental Income	$18,000	$20,867	$24,190	$28,043	$32,510
Principal & Interest	$9,276	$9,276	$9,276	$9,276	$9,276
Tax & Insurance	$2,740[*]	$3,176	$3,682	$4,269	$4,949
Property Mgmt Fees	$1,440	$1,669	$1,935	$2,243	$2,600
Annual Profit	$4,544	$6,746	$9,297	$12,255	$15,685
Property Value	$185,400	$208,669	$241,905	$280,434	$325,100
Mortgage Balance	$141,876	$132,234	$117,133	$97,754	$72,884
Gross Equity	$43,524	$76,435	$124,772	$182,680	$252,216

The increase in rental income, tax & insurance, property management and property value has been calculated using a 3% annual rate (I use a 3% rate in this example and have used 4% in another example. This is to illustrate that these are merely examples, and the rate can vary.) For simplicity, HOA (if any) and unexpected costs (repairs/vacancy), were not calculated in this example.

Yes, you may possibly get some immediate positive cash flow when you first buy and rent because interest rates are low, property taxes are low, or you got a great price when you bought, but these are secondary considerations. You'll see in the next section that focusing too much on those things instead of the main reasons we buy single-family homes (so inflation can erode the 30-year loan as your tenants pay it off and the property builds valuable equity as a long-term investment) leads some people to become investment casualties.

How to avoid becoming a short-term thinking casualty

I've shown you that real estate shows its power in the long term. Yet there's a lot of noise out there, confusing people into thinking otherwise. Let's look at the mistakes I've seen people make so you can avoid becoming one of three types of casualties: interest rate, market discount, and cash flow. I've seen people who were so righteous about these things that they literally bought *nothing*.

Interest rate casualties

Interest rate casualties are the people who fixate on interest rates. They say things like, "the interest rate is higher than it was last year/last quarter/last month so it's too late to buy." They get upset that they're being quoted a 3.875% interest rate instead of the 3.75% they wanted to get. Frankly, these interest rate casualties are staring at short-term trees and cannot see the beautiful, vast, long-term forest ahead.

When I started investing, interest rates were high enough that I typically experienced negative cash flow at the beginning of the process. Now interest rates are so low that positive cash flow situations are possible. And yet, that's not the point.

A real-life example is useful here because I've seen too many people get myopic about this. I really don't want you to become an interest rate casualty.

In early 2018, I received an email from a person asking me, "How can I make a profit on a 5.125% loan? I previously got a 4.6% loan."

He was clearly thinking only about immediate short-term profit instead of the long-term, lifelong benefits that may positively impact his financial future (take a look at the chart in the previous section again). This gentleman was meeting with his financial advisor, so he was saying things like, "How can I make $300 per month net?" and "I should make 5% on any cash I put in." I understood where he was coming from. I've found that typically financial advisors are not necessarily familiar with the benefits of investing in single-family rental homes, powered by the 30-year fixed-rate loan. Many can be biased toward what they are familiar with—securities, even if those don't earn commissions for them. Single-family home rentals are typically not on their investment radar.

I share this with you because many people are led into thinking short-term like this gentleman, to the detriment of their long-term financial future. Here's how I responded to him while sharing the critical expertise he was missing

This note to the investor was written in 2018:

I think you are forgetting the larger context here. My thrust to buy single-family homes as rentals and hold them began when interest rates were at 14%. Even then, it still made sense to buy. Yes, cash flow started out at a negative at 14% interest, but since the loan was fixed and never ever changed with inflation while rents did increase, it eventually, after some years, got to a breakeven point. From that point on, I knew my future was set. Of course, with more time, more homes started becoming positive.

When rates were 8% we were ecstatic—properties actually started out at essentially a breakeven point, then got more and more positive as the years went by, rents went up, but the mortgage (principal and interest portion) of the payment never changed!

In the past decade, rates have been the lowest in the past 50-60 years! Yes, the very lowest point was about 1.5 years ago when investor rates were at 4.5% (remember, investors always get rates that are higher than homeowners). However, even with rates going up slightly and being in the 5.25%-5.5% range or so now, they are still some of the lowest and most amazing rates in history. 5.125% is an astoundingly good rate!

I am refinancing some homes now and the rate I am getting as an investor on a government refi is 5.5%. I am grabbing it!

Historically, over my career, 7.5% was considered a great rate. I would grab that magical 5.125% and run with it! While rates may go up or down in the coming years, this is already a very low point in the history of mortgage interest rates.

Remember, you are buying these homes so your future gets stronger. When you have a 30-year fixed-rate loan, where the payment and the balance never keep up with inflation, it makes your future very strong.

We'll talk this week. Until then, grab these loans! At least that's what I would do. — Adiel

After I wrote that response, I thought about the hundreds of people I had already seen retire, like my friend Brad (whose success story I feature to end this chapter). Brad bought 16 homes in Phoenix with us in the 90s. His rates back then? Between 7% and 8%. It made no difference. When rates got down to 6.5%, he refinanced. Inflation eroded the real buying power and real value of his payments and loans until the loans were so small, he just paid them off to own the homes free and clear. Now he's just enjoying early retirement with multiple, steady streams of rental income that increase annually with inflation.

I thought about the homes I bought when rates were 14% and I think, "I wish I had bought more of them." The interest rate didn't matter in the long term.

Happily, I was able to speak with the gentleman who emailed me, worried about the 5.125% interest rate. He indeed closed on that loan. He avoided becoming an interest rate casualty. My guess is he'll be a very happy camper in five years—ecstatic in ten.

Market discount casualties

The people who become market discount casualties say things like, "I went to a boot camp and learned I must buy properties only below market price. I should never pay the market price."

While I cannot fault anyone for wanting to buy at a discount, I want you to be wary of those who say "you *only* make money when you *buy* a property." That sentence could doom your financial future. That philosophy could lead you to buy cheap properties in declining neighborhoods that look good on paper but are, in fact, expensive disasters. Or worse.

I've seen someone walk away from a fine investment priced at $140,000 because he offered $130,000 (believing "never pay market price") and of course ended up not buying it because the seller sold it for the fair market price to another buyer. People who think this way frequently end up buying nothing...but at least they're very righteous about their opinion.

Discount casualties might be so fixated they fail to see that sometimes an entire metropolitan area or even an entire state could be a "bargain." Buying "low" doesn't necessarily mean lower than market price. It means a market is low *overall* compared to other markets.

If you truly believe at this moment that you'll *only* make money when you buy, I hope you're changing your mind as you soak in these tips. If not, you'll be hitting yourself in the forehead in the coming years, wishing you had listened to my advice. You'll wish you listened to other investors who have shared their stories throughout this book. You'll wish you had bought single-family homes for yourself. You'll see in the next chapter our best practices for where and what to buy for the long term.

Cash flow casualties

The third casualty category I call cash flow casualties. I'm not exaggerating when I say that I hear this from every foreigner investing in the U.S. It doesn't matter who I meet. Sometimes it's a couple making $600,000 annually in Silicon Valley who truly don't need additional monthly cash flow at this time. It could be a billionaire in any country.

It sounds like this: "I hear you're helping people buy in the United States. What's my yield?" or "How much cash flow will I get? I saw in the newspaper that you can get a 12% yield in Detroit."

Do you know what this short-term thinking causes cash flow casualties to do? They buy in crime-ridden neighborhoods, in declining markets, chasing a short-term yield. Ten years later, as their friend who listened to my advice and experience is sending their child to college and getting ready to retire with a solid net worth, that poor cash flow casualty is experiencing the opposite. Why? Because that 12% yield they were intent on capturing was for one or two years. After that, they couldn't rent the property profitab lyagain and might have even lost the home in foreclosure because the market might have tanked.

I'm helping you avoid the major landmines I see in this industry. These three types of casualties really hurt people. These teachings confuse and derail people from ever buying any rental properties. They encourage people to buy the wrong types of properties and the landmines blow up.

Here's a fun example to see how important it is to buy with long-term thinking and not become a short-term casualty. Imagine you're standing in Palo Alto, California, where the median home price is now around $2,900,000 in 2021. Now imagine you got access to a time machine to go back to late 1970s Palo Alto, just as the first *Star Wars* movie was being released. All around, you see new homes for sale at a market value of $100,000.

Are you really **not** going to buy homes in Palo Alto for $100,000 each if the 30-year fixed-rate loan you're offered is at 14% interest because your friend got a loan for 13.2%? Are you going to let these properties go to some other investor because you were advised to buy *only* at a discount below market price to make money when you buy? Are you going to miss out on the tremendous equity growth and income-producing benefits of these homes because the cash flow is a little bit negative to start? Are you going to say, "Take me back to 2021; I'm not buying any of these homes at market value."? Of course not.

See how ridiculous this is? Do you see how much you hurt your future self by not buying as many homes as possible for $100,000 or even $120,000 in 1977–homes worth $2,900,000 each in 2021?

The minute you begin to think long-term and understand what's in this chapter, that's when you become independent of the cyclical booms/busts that inevitably happen in our economy. That's when you'll take action to start investing. It's like you have been granted access to a time machine. You can see into the future decades ahead and see your portfolio of single-family homes (financed with 30-year fixed-rate loans and being paid for by your tenants) is taking care of you. You'll prevent the dent in your forehead from the "woulda, coulda, shoulda" hits that will sadly be experienced by those who became casualties.

What you owe today, you own tomorrow

As we end this chapter, it's best to remember that mantra: what you owe today, you *own* tomorrow. That phrase keeps you from thinking about immediate, short-term profit and helps you focus on the long-term, lifelong, net worth, future income-producing benefits we've outlined here. You'll take action to start buying single-family homes instead of becoming an interest rate, market discount, or cash flow casualty who bought nothing, or worse, bought the wrong properties.

If you follow this advice and invest for the long term to allow inflation to do its magic year after year as tenants pay down your 30-year fixed-rate loan, the home(s) you'll eventually own free and clear can become cornerstones of your net worth and key building blocks for your financial future. Any time you doubt this and get consumed by short-term thinking, please review the Long-Term Investment Profits chart in this chapter.

Let's end this chapter with an analogy: time is your ally in buying single-family homes, just as it is in baking a cake. To bake a cake, you need to put together the ingredients, mix them up, put the batter in the baking pan, heat the oven and then what? You need the right amount of time. Time is what the cake *needs*. You want to make a cake in three minutes? It's going to be terrible. On the contrary, let it bake for the required 35 minutes and you'll have a great cake. The same idea applies when buying single-family homes. Give the loans the time inflation needs to make them deliciously satisfying for you.

ECOSYSTEM BENEFIT
Market Intelligence for the Long-Term

"When you're buying single-family homes in communities far from where you live, it's smart to buy through an entity that truly knows the market inside and out. In the 27 years I've been investing following Adiel's expertise, I've seen him build a solid infrastructure that's connected with local real estate brokers and property managers who know the good neighborhoods and the ones to avoid. This local knowledge is indispensable both before and after you decide to buy.

"For example, I once owned twelve rental homes in Phoenix. One home was in a neighborhood that began to decline, something I wouldn't have known, living in California. Fortunately, my property manager alerted me to this change. She suggested I consider selling this house. She had been an excellent property manager, so I chose her as my broker to sell it. It sold at double the original price. This insight and support from someone in the ICG ecosystem proved very valuable to me."
—Brad H., ICG client since 1991, who began investing in his early thirties and now owns ten single-family homes in Phoenix, two in San Antonio, and two in Oklahoma City

INVESTOR STORY
In His Own Words

In 1991, 31-year-old Brad had a good friend who had attended one of ICG's quarterly Expos. She was considering buying a single-family home to rent. She invited Brad, for moral support, to join her for a coffee shop meeting she had scheduled with me. Brad's friend decided to purchase a home in Scottsdale, Arizona. Brad was intrigued by the discussion and decided to buy a few homes in Phoenix. In fact, Brad purchased five homes between May and October that year. Within three years of buying that initial group of homes, Brad purchased four more single-family homes in the Phoenix area.

I asked him to summarize his experiences over the last 27 years. Here's what he shared:

"I have concluded that buying single-family homes is a great, secure long-term investment. Throughout the years, I've played in the stock market and done very mediocre. It's my real estate investments that have done well. I've seen that most people who truly invest for the *long-term* do not lose money investing in single-family homes. I've heard about people flipping homes who make money, but I believe that's risky, and you've got to get lucky.

57

"What I learned from Adiel about keeping assets for the long term that has directly affected me is this: My rental home investments have appreciated greatly in value since the 1990s. And I've seen the crashes. In one downturn, I had a lot of vacancies and evictions. I estimated a $50,000 negative cash flow in one year. I've learned that it's difficult to collect money after an eviction and never actually have done so; you can't get blood from a stone. I saw the value of my properties more than double during the "bubble," only to get cut in half during the big downturn of 2008. Since then, they have slowly returned to new highs. Yet, through the long-term, 27 years later, this nest egg keeps on giving.

"Let's talk about the booms. Those have been terrific! One of the fortunate things I did was sell a home in Scottsdale at the peak of the bubble. I had purchased it for $109K in the 1990s. It wasn't renting well, and it had a pool. I sensed it might be a good time to sell it. It sold quickly for triple what I had paid for it. In retrospect, it turned out to be the peak of the bubble. My timing was lucky.

"I used the large gains from that sale to buy two new homes in Oklahoma City. So, I effectively traded a well-appreciated property with bad cash flow in Arizona for two new properties with good cash flow in Oklahoma. Both of those homes have also experienced normal, gradual appreciation in an excellent rental market.

"In retrospect, if I did this all over again, I wouldn't buy fewer houses and I certainly wouldn't buy cheaper houses. I would've bought more homes in the types of good, middle-class neighborhoods that Adiel's network shows us. Adiel's ecosystem never shows us homes in undesirable neighborhoods.

"In fact, after I became an experienced investor with several properties in different markets, I decided to venture beyond good, middle-class neighborhoods and invest in a few even higher quality homes. I wish I had done more of that after getting my feet wet.

"My story is one of buying and thinking long-term: I've been able to pay off the mortgages on almost all of my properties. As of early 2018, only four of the fourteen properties are not yet fully paid off, meaning I have a very positive cash flow. This collection of single-family homes has become my main nest egg. Adiel's guidance and assistance has had a profound effect on me. It enabled me to enjoy a semi-retirement. I've cut back my hours and I'm off the regular schedule at the hospital. I work now only to stay engaged.

"Lastly, I've realized something important. Psychologically, when you have a big retirement nest egg, a solid portfolio, you definitely don't want to get to the point where you're whittling it down, especially so if you decide to retire early. The beauty of having a retirement portfolio of assets that pay you is this: my rental income goes into my checking account; the physical real estate assets are my retirement portfolio for my future. I'm definitely not whittling that away. I feel very positive about what I've done and I'm so happy that I did it keeping the long-term view in mind."

REPLAY

- **Properly buying, renovating and selling properties (aka "flipping") is usually a full-time job done by professionals.**

- **In the short term, markets fluctuate. Over the long term, they steadily go up, rising on average 1.5 times the cost of living.**

- **You don't have to chart the markets, just stay in for the long term.**

- **Short-term profits rely on luck and timing, like gambling.**

- **Even if you speculate, you must be prepared to hold on to the property for the long term.**

- **Real estate really shows its power over the long term.**

- **Long-term investment thinking and action prevents the inaction suffered by interest rate casualties, market discount casualties, and cash flow casualties.**

- **What you owe today, you own tomorrow.**

CHAPTER 4

Best Practices on Where and What to Buy

"It is infinitely better to buy a good home than not to buy the very best home. This is also true for where you buy. It is infinitely better to buy a home in a good market than not to buy a home in the very best market." — *Adiel Gorel*

I'm going to start this chapter with an example of two investors who first did the *opposite* of the advice I'm going to share with you now. This happened long before they learned what you're about to learn here, and long before they joined the ICG ecosystem. It's important to do this to clearly distinguish my approach and experience from other techniques you'll encounter in the industry (some of which, quite frankly, could ruin you financially). These two clients were kind enough to share the painful details of their story, hoping, as I do too, that many others will avoid the pain they've endured. I'm very grateful to them for having done so.

Let's meet Sheila and Dave, a couple who began investing in the stock market three decades ago, as young engineers in their early thirties. As single professionals, each had purchased a primary residence. When they got married, they sold both properties and moved together to a larger home.

In their fifties, in an effort to diversify their investments beyond the stock market, they bought their first single-family home rental in 2009 in Santa Clara, California. Sheila's parents had passed away; she used cash from the inheritance to pay for this first rental. One year later, they purchased another rental, this one in San Jose, also for cash.

Sheila said, "We didn't want to have 30-year mortgages for rental properties because back then, we thought we shouldn't have mortgages for anything other than our primary residence."

They sold both of those houses in 2011, which Sheila now realizes wasn't a good idea. Those properties have since appreciated tremendously.

Looking at their looming retirement scenario, in 2016, they attended an expensive real estate boot camp with an organization selling tools to analyze properties. Sheila and Dave were encouraged to buy cheap houses, well below market rate, seeking short-term gains via "flipping" as many have heard about on TV. This is how Sheila described their investing experience after that boot camp:

> "We started looking at a neighborhood in Detroit that the seminar speaker had suggested we analyze. One home was offered to us at the seminar for $50,000. They claimed it was 'a fully rehabbed house with a renter in place.'"

They signed the contract to purchase that house.

> "When we got home, we read the inspection report we paid for and did some market research," said Sheila. "We found that same home listed for $30,000 and realized what was happening. We backed out of the contract."

That same still-vacant house showed up on the realtor multiple listings months later and they contracted to buy it for $30,000.

> Sheila said, "It took a long time to get that house unencumbered from the mess it was in. In fact, we found the next four houses we wanted and completed those four purchases before closing on that first house. Too bad we didn't see that as a huge red flag! We had more rehab work to do before renting that first house. That's been the case with most of our Detroit houses."

Later on, they paid cash for five more properties in Detroit.

> "Looking back, we learned that when you're buying cheaper properties like these, it's difficult to get a loan," shared Dave. "We used up a lot of our cash right away buying those nine small, cheap homes. Plus, we didn't know how neglected the properties were."

> Sheila added, "The blight there is real. In fact, the city has clamped down and is now requiring two annual inspections: one inspecting for livability and the second for 'lead clearance.' That second inspection costs us $500 per house, plus a $150 management company fee to supervise each inspection. Then we have to submit these inspection reports to the city."

After paying a lot for that flipping boot camp training, they've had to pump a lot more cash into upgrading those properties.

Dave shared that, "Even now, all nine of those supposedly cheap properties are at zero cash flow. The equity growth is good but still no cash flow."

Sheila added, "What did we learn in Detroit? We learned how expensive it is to lose a tenant in the middle of winter. We understand now how pricey it can be to secure the home because it's not in a good neighborhood. We had to pay to winterize the home. Then we paid again to open up the home and get it ready to rent in the spring. We know what it's like to lose half a year's rent after having spent all that money. These are very expensive lessons."

Reflecting on Sheila and Dave's story, I think you can see why when I was offered similar properties in Detroit, properties that didn't meet the best practices criteria I'm going to describe in this chapter, I said, "No, thank you."

Upon hearing their story, our mutual friend Larry, who I've known for many years, said: "Come with me to an ICG Expo and learn a different way." At the end of this chapter, you can learn how their story has come to a much brighter spot.

Before we get to that, I'm going to teach you the advice thousands of busy people have used to set in motion powerful financial futures. I'm going to teach you where to buy in the U.S. and what to buy as well.

The best practices I encourage clients to follow are these: Buy single-family homes in large metropolitan areas located within Sun Belt states. Buy in those metro areas in communities with strong economic diversity (meaning a variety of industries producing a wide variety of jobs). Within those areas, choose nice (but not too fancy) neighborhoods, and focus on purchasing new or newish homes with three or four bedrooms and two baths, from a builder when possible. We'll break down the reasoning behind this formula I've used for decades in the rest of this chapter.

Why large metropolitan areas?

Why buy in large metro areas instead of in smaller towns? One reason. Have you ever heard about life in a small town dominated by one factory? Can you imagine owning homes in a small town when that major employer suddenly closes, and all those employees lose their paychecks? Smaller towns with few employers can have major negative consequences for you as an investor during a big economic downturn.

On the contrary, large metro areas typically have much more economic diversity, a variety of industries, maybe a university or two, perhaps a military installation or large complex of federal buildings. The loss of one or two employers won't devastate the entire community like it does in small towns. So that's why we choose to invest in large metro areas.

It's a huge country —
Baby Boomer retirees are on the move

I've been a student of U.S. demographics since I began my investment career over 30 years ago. The U.S. Census tells us what states are gaining population at the fastest clip. There is one reason to pay attention to demographics before buying single-family homes to use as rentals: Baby Boomers. This group is comprised of a huge number of Americans (somewhere around 77 million) who were born between 1946 and 1964, of which I am one. For the older group, retirement has already begun. Many of them are relocating to the Sun Belt states. In the next dozen years or so, there will continue to be a wave of Baby Boomer retirees—the largest such demographic change in American history. Many of these retirees will likely head to Sun Belt states too, as has been the historical pattern for decades.

As Americans age, northern tier states will probably gain population at a significantly slower rate than the Sun Belt States; the Sun Belt is where demographic changes look to be potentially strongest. Why? Retirees desire good weather, lower state tax rates, and lower cost of living. Some Sun Belt states like Texas, Nevada, and Florida have no income tax. There are also northern states like Wyoming, South Dakota, and Washington State that have no income tax. However, none of them are on our radar as potential investment markets. Wyoming and South Dakota have no large metropolitan areas, while the large metro areas in Washington are way too expensive for us to invest in 2018. Plus, as investors, we seek a pro-business/pro-landlord environment and markets that are not yet booming.

Why the Sun Belt states?

What do I mean by the Sun Belt? Generally speaking, if you look at a map of the U.S., it's the states from Nevada to Florida. In 2021, our ICG investors are buying single-family homes mostly in Oklahoma, Florida, and North Carolina. Before this, we invested in Nevada, Arizona, Texas, and other states as well.

Weather: If you're approaching 70 years of age, do you want to take your winter walks in Chicago when it's five degrees below zero outside or enjoy the January sun in Central Florida when it's 70 degrees? Most retirees would choose the latter, and demographic movements prove this preference towards the sun.

Lower cost of living (including state income taxes): Not only does this swath of country enjoy lower costs for food, gasoline, and housing, but many of these states also have low state income tax rates. Some of these states even charge no state income tax! So, this makes Sun Belt states attractive even to people who aren't retirees. For retirees, when paychecks stop coming and you're living on a fixed income receiving social security checks (as so many Americans do), this lower cost-of-living causes many retirees to head for the Sun Belt to stretch their retirement income.

A pro-business environment: Businesses are naturally attracted to pro-business states. This is a business culture with less taxation and less regulation; political leaders put mechanisms in place to attract new industries and employers. In this type of environment, especially in states gaining in population numbers as Baby Boomers age, this means a higher likelihood that new construction will continue. In a pro-business state, these criteria also mean state laws favor landlords over tenants.

If you were wondering why California was left out of the description above, not being pro-business is one big reason. California has lots of regulations and taxation. For someone looking to buy investment properties to rent, California is a state whose laws are very favorable to tenants, not landlords. Evictions can take up to and even over a year in California—a long time to feel like someone is stealing money from you if they stop paying rent and you still have to pay the mortgage. Additionally, home price vs. rental income ratios in California, at press time, are very out-of-whack: prices are high while rents, as a percentage of price, are very low compared to other Sun Belt markets. California, while technically in the Sun Belt, fails most of the critical criteria, so we go east instead.

A not-yet booming market: When I go visit a market to assess it, if the realtor tells me the market is "booming," I tell the agent that's not what I like to hear. I'm a buyer. I want to buy in a market that isn't yet booming. I want to buy where homes are reasonably priced. For me, this typically means single-family homes are priced under $350,000 or even under $250,000, and the market hasn't experienced huge growth recently. These criteria also help us choose where within a metro city to look to buy. Of course, during the COVID-19 pandemic, home prices in most cities have increased quite rapidly. Rents have also increased, but rents typically increase slower than home prices. However, interest rates have dropped during the pandemic, to the lowest point in history. These low rates create lower mortgage payments, which makes the increasing prices still affordable from a cash-flow standpoint. In addition, as of mid-2021, inflation is starting to rear its head. Getting a 30-year fixed rate loan, heading into higher inflation, is actually very beneficial for the savvy rental home buyer.

A good white-collar neighborhood: We focus on a certain type of neighborhood to be part of the American Dream. People want to live in the type of home they've imagined in a comfortable neighborhood. We don't invest in run-down neighborhoods for the reasons outlined in the opening story of this chapter; we also don't invest where the neighborhood is too fancy because typically the numbers won't work. Which leads to the last item...

Evaluate good rental income compared to the purchase price: We don't want to buy in markets where the rents are too low relative to the purchase price. We want the rental incomes to be at a good ratio compared to the purchase price. Here's an example: Suppose there's a home priced at $250,000 that rents at $1,850/month. That sounds pretty good, right? There's a secondary question to ask: What are the property taxes here? If this home is in a high property tax market, the $1850 monthly rent might not be so enticing. It might be equal in value to a home that rents for $1450 in a market with low property taxes. See how that works? If the $1850 rent is in a market with low property taxes, now *that* is a good rental income relative to the purchase price, and the numbers work. Of course, when mortgage rates are extremely low, as they are in 2021, that makes cash flow better, as if rents were higher during regular interest rate periods.

What to buy

Okay, so now we're in the Sun Belt, in a large metro area, looking at a variety of nice white-collar neighborhoods. What do we wish to buy here? What have I found works well?

A true American Dream — single-family homes

Single-family homes are at the heart of the American Dream. Many people want the picket fence, the yard, and the two-car garage. More than any other type of real estate, single-family homes are always in demand, and are therefore the most liquid. As an investment, they're the most stable. As a piece of property, they're the easiest to rent, maintain, manage, and sell. For busy investors, quality single-family homes located in good neighborhoods offer the most effortless, stress-free real estate investment possible, with the best appreciation potential. Plus, single-family homes typically rent to families with kids who are in school (a trait that can act as an anchor, keeping the family in place for years). This creates a more stable tenant dynamic for investors.

Single-family homes are the best investment in terms of liquidity, financing, and ease of management. From experience, I know single-family homes are the safest, easiest, and most dependable real estate investment you can make. Single-family homes generate the financial benefits that will secure your future without the hassles many other types of property entail. However, I stress that the only kind of single-family homes to buy are *quality* single-family homes, located in good neighborhoods.

What do I mean by "quality" single-family homes?

I mean a house that's reasonably new (if possible, brand-new) and in good structural condition. One that's aesthetically appealing, has a well-tended, functional yard, a garage, two baths, and at least three bedrooms. It doesn't have to be a showplace or the house of your dreams—in fact, it probably shouldn't be. But it should be a place where a family can live comfortably.

What about other types of investments I've heard about?

Let me address this question with a story, which (unfortunately) does not have a happy ending. About twenty- five years ago, an elderly woman I knew called and asked me to come to her home in the elegant Seacliff neighborhood in San Francisco. Her home had Pacific Ocean and Golden Gate Bridge views—a very special property. I knew she had been investing in some kind of real estate somewhere (and not through us). She called me frantically because she was desperate to sell her lovely home. She asked me to buy it for $1.2 million. Knowing the market value was actually $1.6 million at the time, I asked why she was so motivated to sell her beautiful home. Despondent, she answered, "Because the 24-unit apartment building I bought in Santa Cruz has wiped me out."

Not wanting to take advantage of her situation, I chose not to buy her home in Seacliff. I can speculate, but still wonder what terrible luck befell her with that apartment building. How terrible things had to be for her to practically beg to sell her amazing home, well below market value, in one of San Francisco's most beautiful neighborhoods. It's a heartbreaking story.

Your story can have a much happier ending.

If quality single-family homes are such a great investment, you may be wondering, why haven't the other books you've read told you the same thing?

For one, buying a single-family home isn't the most exciting investment. It doesn't have the same *caché* as, for instance, purchasing an apartment complex or a mini-mall. But along with bragging rights, go a lot of headaches. I've tried those other kinds of investments, yet I've made the most (and easiest) money with single-family homes, the least "macho" real estate.

Do I care? Not at all.

Another reason you don't hear continuous buzz about quality single-family homes is that often they have the worst cash flow—at first glance. When you look at older, lower-quality single-family homes in older, lower-quality neighborhoods, their cash flow seems better. As an example, a $90,000 house that rents for $1,000 is more profitable (on paper) than a $240,000 house that rents for $1800. So why do I continue to recommend quality single-family homes?

Because cash flow on paper doesn't tell the whole story. Older, low-quality properties require more repairs and often tenant turnover is more frequent. These things not only cost you money, but time. (Remember the story of Sheila and Dave's expensive lessons learned in Detroit at the beginning of this chapter.) In addition, a low-quality home won't necessarily appreciate as rapidly as a high-quality home.

In comparison, quality single-family homes attract good, stable tenants who usually pay their rent on time and typically don't damage your property. These elements help make your investment work.

Remember, you're investing for the long-term. A quality single-family home will likely continue to rise in value, and your rental income will increase with the cost of living.

In the example on the next page, first year figures show a before-tax profit of $3919. After adding in tax savings from the depreciation deduction, the property shows a net profit of $3919, as the depreciation more than covered the profit (in fact there is a small additional loss remaining which can be used elsewhere). Each year, as rental rates increase, positive cash flow also increases. The example refers to a $200,000 house rented for $1,600 a month. The loan is 80% of the house value, at an interest rate of 4%. All expenses are assumed to increase by 3% per year. Marginal tax used was 32%.

$200,000 SINGLE-FAMILY HOME 5-YEAR CASH FLOW FIGURES					
	Year 1	Year 2	Year 3	Year 4	Year 5
Rental Income	$19,200	$19,776	$20,369	$20,980	$21,610
Principal & Interest	$9,166	$9,166	$9,166	$9,166	$9,166
Tax & Insurance	$3,082	$3,174	$3,270	$3,368	$3,469
Misc. Expenses	$1,800	$1,854	$1,910	$1,976	$2,026
Gross Profit (Loss)	$5,152	$5,582	$6,023	$6,479	$6,949
Depreciation Deduction	$5,818	$5,818	$5,818	$5,818	$5,818
Net Profit	$5,152	$5,582	$5,957	$6,267	$6,587

More best practices and criteria for buying single-family homes

As much as possible, I suggest you buy *new* homes with a builder's warranty. Why? Because when you buy this way, all the systems in the home are under warranty, decreasing the probability you'll need to spend cash on home repairs in the first few years. New homes mean new pipes underground too—something you might overlook if buying cheaper older homes at severely discounted prices. So, focus on finding new homes when possible.

How big? The typical American family who rents a home wants three or four bedrooms with two baths. That's the highly desirable sweet spot for families who rent. The home size should be between 1200 sf and 2400 sf (with 1300 sf to 1800 sf being most common). If this sounds too specific, it's by design. If the home is too tiny or too huge, you're buying a home that will appeal to a subset of renters instead of to the majority of potential tenants in the types of communities we've described.

And while we're on that topic, I must add this advice because I don't want you to fall into a common trap: when buying single-family homes to serve your financial needs as rentals, please, please do not insert your biases as a homeowner into the process. I once knew a man who insisted on spending thousands of dollars to convert an all-electric kitchen to gas because that was his preference as a homeowner. His potential tenants wanted an all-electric kitchen—it's what they expected in that city. Think of it this way: feel free to decorate your home as you want—with pine tree knots on the banisters, antlers in the kitchen, whatever look you like. Trust me when I say to keep eccentric styles and oddities out of your rental homes to maintain a broad appeal for the rental market. Listen to your local broker about styles and colors that will appeal to the people you want to attract as tenants.

Lastly, when you're looking to buy your first single-family home, keep in mind that this isn't an exact science. You'll logically spend the most time doing the analysis to buy your first single-family home rental. That's the point of this book: to impart knowledge so you'll understand the best practices we know have worked for thousands of investors focused on building long-term wealth. We hope to give you enough information and comfort to be ready to buy your first single-family home rental within six months or less of reading this book.

We want you to start buying good homes with a 30-year fixed-rate loan and use local property management firms to make your life easier. Get it done and then you can think about buying rental home number two (which will be simpler). You'll understand the reasoning behind the advice I've shared here and the entire process. By the time you're ready to buy your third, fourth, and fifth single-family home to rent, you'll almost be bored. You *want* it to be boring and easy.

ECOSYSTEM BENEFIT
Local know-how when learning where and what to buy

"I was ready to buy my first rental property in Arizona. Adiel connected me with a real estate broker there who was extremely knowledgeable about a variety of locations, the nature of different developments, the range of market rate rents, the different types of homes being built, the relative ease or difficulty of being able to rent the properties—all of it. He also made those helpful one-pagers showing property pricing, characteristics, and cash flow projections. This relationship was extremely valuable to me. I didn't have to do any of that time-consuming research because Adiel had done the work to bring this expertise into the ICG infrastructure."—*Jack, ICG investor since the 1990s, who began investing in the 1980s in his early forties; today he owns several units in the Bay Area and over a dozen rental homes in the greater Phoenix area*

INVESTOR STORY
In His Own Words

Don't worry, I didn't forget about the couple we met at the beginning of the chapter. If you remember, they were investing in cheap homes in

Detroit—with devastating results. When we left the story, their friend Larry said to them: "Come with me to an ICG Expo, meet Adiel, and learn a different way to think about and buy single-family homes."

Dave and Sheila have been coming to ICG events for nearly two years now with Larry. They've begun to invest for the long-term—for their retirement. Dave has already retired; Sheila is planning on retiring in the next few years.

> Sheila said, "Now, we're buying new homes in the Oklahoma City area. We now better understand we should harness the inflation-fighting power of 30-year fixed-rate mortgages for our rental properties. We're in a hurry to get a couple of mortgages while we qualify before I retire, and the paychecks stop."

And those nine houses in Detroit they've spent "a fortune" on since 2016?

> Sheila says, "We plan to sell those. We've gained some equity in a few of them, not all. The biggest house has almost appreciated to the point that we think we'll break even for the whole thing there."

Sheila and Dave are well on their way to adding single-family home investments to the retirement portfolio they first started building with stocks when they were in their 30s. They've also added alternative investments in recent years, so they feel well diversified.

> Sheila said, "Single-family homes will provide us the steady income we're seeking for the long-term as retirees once we stop receiving regular paychecks. The rental income and equity increases going forward will be more productive for us than most of the other investments we've made so far."

> Dave added, "Now we know that if we buy new homes, it's actually better for the short and the long term. It's so much better than buying old houses with old pipes. Adiel really tells the truth. Going forward, we'll purchase more new homes.

We're planning on buying a new duplex too. We learned in Detroit that buying low-priced houses uses up a lot of your cash. You don't enjoy any leverage. Lesson learned."

"Lastly," said [Dave], "Adiel's advice about where and what to buy is excellent. He also encourages buyers to go to the communities where you're buying. See the actual location and property with your own eyes. Talk to the developer. Meet the property manager. Get a real feel for the community where you'll be owning this rental home. In Detroit, we didn't do that. We bought those properties sight unseen. I feel we probably wouldn't have purchased them if I'd gone there to see for myself. So now, we're following Adiel's advice and have decided to invest in Oklahoma. We're buying a single-family home in early 2018 and plan to also buy a new duplex there."

REPLAY

Single-family homes are the best investment for the individual investor in terms of:

- liquidity,
- financing,
- ease of management, and potential appreciation.
- Quality single-family homes are best for long-term investments.
- Don't confuse cash flow with quality.
- A property's cash flow usually improves over time.
- Remember to include tax benefits, if any, into cash flow figures.
- New homes in metro areas with economic diversity in Sun Belt states are recommended.

CHAPTER 5

How I've Seen People Raise or Access Cash to Buy Single-Family Homes

In *Remote Control Retirement Riches,* I provided eight ways I have seen busy people raise cash to buy single-family home rentals. Here they are, plus a few more:

Earn it

Save it

Have the feds help you save

Sell unused assets

Borrow it

- Refinance or get an equity loan against a property
- Borrow against 401(k), Roth IRA or Traditional IRA
- From friends or relatives
- From a bank
- From credit cards (beware!!!)
- Partner with a friend who is cash-rich but time-poor
- Buy through a different entity altogether, such as a self-directed IRA

Earn it

For many busy people, adding part-time employment to earn more money is usually out of the question. For some, perhaps at-home work for an Internet marketing company or a side hobby, or creating a podcast in your area of expertise could produce several hundred (or thousands) of dollars a month. Perhaps you have expertise that's in demand and can work several evenings each month as a consultant in your field. If you have few assets and an income that's already stretched to the limit, a part-time business may be your answer. You'll enjoy the additional revenue—and tax deductions against your income, which may lead to tax savings. (Ask your tax preparer how this may apply to your particular situation.)

Save it

You may wonder why you're finding it hard to save, even after you get a raise. You're not alone. On average, in the U.S., people are saving only 2.4% of their after-tax income. Learning to budget and allocate funds for your future is essential to becoming financially fit. In fact, the money you set aside for investments is the most important part of your budget. To make a profound difference in your future, you must reorganize your priorities. You should place investment funds right up there with food, shelter, and insurance.

There's only one way to save more without earning more money, and that's to spend less. Your spending habits are the first place to look for cash. Collect all your receipts from the past three months (if you're self-employed, or have a fluctuating income, you may want to go back six months). Use that information to fill out the form on the following page or make up a list or spreadsheet of your own. Evaluating your spending is probably the most painful part of the process; it's also one of the most enlightening. Most people are shocked when they realize just how much they spend each month on things that aren't exactly necessary.

Looking over your expenditures, you're sure to find areas where you can economize. It may be time to bite the bullet and trade off some of the luxuries you enjoy now—frequent dining out or expensive vacations—

in order to begin building your future. Only when you stop to analyze where your money has gone can you begin to take action to reduce the outflow. Then you can decide to pay yourself first, putting money into a fund you'll eventually use to buy single-family homes.

EXPENDITURES WORKSHEET

Mortgage or Rent _____

Property Tax _____

Homeowners/Renters Insurance _____

Utilities _____

Furnishings, Maintenance _____

Phone and Internet _____

Other Household Expenses _____

Groceries _____

Dining Out _____

Car Loan/Lease _____

Fuel, Maintenance & Repairs _____

Auto Insurance _____

Other Transportation (taxi, bus, etc.) _____

Federal, State, Local Taxes _____

Social Security/Pension Contributions _____

Tax on Investment Income _____

Retirement Plan Contributions _____

Passbook/Money Market Savings _____

Health Insurance _____

Medical Services, Drugs not covered by insurance _____

Health Club Dues _____

Child Care _____

Movies, Theater, Cable TV _____

Books, Magazines, Videos _____

Apparel, Shoes _____

Personal Care (haircuts, massage) _____

Laundry, Dry Cleaning _____

Vacations, Travel _____

Miscellaneous Expenses _____

TOTAL MONTHLY EXPENSES $ _____

Let the government "force" you to save

If you have a hard time sticking to a budget or tend to spend all your income each month, enlist the government's help. Simply reduce the number of tax exemptions on your W-2 form and more tax dollars will be taken out of each of your paychecks. Months later, you'll get some of it back as a tax refund.

This isn't the best way to save because the feds, not you, earn interest on the money deducted from your earnings. Of course, when you do get your refund, it must go straight into your money market fund or savings account. (In the meantime, put away those credit cards!)

On the other hand, if you receive a large refund each year and are good at leaving a savings account untouched, you may want to increase the number of exemptions on your W-2 form. With more exemptions claimed, fewer tax dollars will be taken out of your paycheck, resulting in a bigger check each pay period. You can put the extra cash you'll receive regularly into your money market fund. You can watch this account grow and earn dividends while you're saving up to buy a single-family home.

Selling unused assets

Earning extra income can be done by selling items you no longer want or need, like that boat or RV that's been gathering dust in the driveway. How about that timeshare you never have time to use? The empty plot of land in Northern Idaho that Uncle Willie left to you? The piano nobody plays?

Take a good look at the things you own. If they're not appreciating assets, and they don't have sentimental value (such as family heirlooms), you might want to consider selling them to raise cash to help you start investing. After all, we're talking about your future. Why let your money sit around in unused assets when it can be working for you?

Borrow it

- From friends or relatives
- Refinance or get an equity loan against a property
- Against 401(k)
- From a bank
- From credit cards (beware!!!)

If you don't have enough cash on hand for a 20% down payment (or a 15% down payment with Private Mortgage Insurance) and you'd like to start investing right away, borrowing may be the answer. The sooner you begin investing, the sooner you'll see benefits, so I always recommend acting as quickly as possible (with some caveats).

There are pros and cons to each of the borrowing methods below. Before you contemplate taking on more debt, take a look at your current obligations. What are your monthly payments? Will you be able to take on an additional monthly payment and still adhere to your new, financially fit budget? If you have credit card debt, are you just paying the minimum every month, or are you able to pay them off in full? If you have a lot of credit card debt, consider consolidating or paying off those debts *before* taking on more debt.

Borrowing from friends or relatives

Approaching a friend or relative with considerable discretionary income and savings may be a fast and easy way to raise the cash you need to get started. If your parents are financially secure, they may be willing to offer you a loan, especially after you've shown them that it'll be used to finance a serious, sound, long-term investment.

Before you begin calling up everyone you know, consider how borrowing money from friends or relatives might affect your relationships. Think about what may happen if, for some reason, you're unable to pay it back. And what if your benefactor suddenly goes broke and needs the money returned right away? As long as everything goes as planned, borrowing from a friend or relative can give you a head start by getting you the down payment you need for your purchase. Chances are they'll offer favorable rates, or even a tax-free gift of up to $15,000 (as of 2021). But unforeseen circumstances do sometimes happen. If you want to maintain good relationships, make sure all parties involved have a complete understanding of the terms of the loan. Put everything in writing: the loan amount, interest rate, and payment schedule. Discuss possibilities that may arise and how you'll deal with them—put those contingency plans in writing, too.

Refinance or get an equity loan against a property

Equity is the difference between your home's current market value and the amount you owe. Your net worth statement should show you how much equity you have in your home, as well as in any rental homes you may own. Assuming you can afford the monthly payments of an equity loan or line, and your current debt load is not too heavy, a home equity loan is perhaps the easiest and most cost-effective way to borrow money from an existing asset. The loan can be against your own residence or against any rental property you own.

Many lenders offer equity loans. Because the loan is secured against your property, interest rates for equity loans are generally lower than rates for unsecured loans. Due to the new tax law of 2018, interest paid on Home Equity Lines of Credit (HELOC) on your own residence may no longer be tax deductible, subject to certain exceptions. This restriction might be lifted as early as 2026. Equity loans against rental properties may have deductible interest. Again, it's best to check with your CPA about your specific situation.

Borrowing from retirement plans

If you have been investing in retirement plans on your own or via your employer, you may find these assets can now become very useful to help you buy single-family homes. Let's review some of these options.

Some plans allow you to borrow money against your retirement account to buy a home; whether or not you can do this is dependent on the plan's custodian. If you've been funding a Roth IRA (meaning you've already paid taxes on those funds), you may be able to take an early distribution against the principal portion you've contributed— not the growth portion –without any penalties. I know this only from seeing people do it. I'm not a CPA, so please consult with yours about any specific accounts.

The advantage of borrowing against your retirement account to raise a down-payment is that you'll be paying back your own account rather than paying interest to a mortgage company. The disadvantage is that if you don't pay the loan back in a specified amount of time, the loan is considered an early distribution. If you're under 59 1/2 years of age, you might have to pay a penalty plus income taxes on the amount borrowed. Please check with your plan custodian so you're clear on the rules and timing.

If you have two retirement accounts, there is another method to consider, which you can think of as buying yourself about four months (beyond the day the home becomes yours) to cover the down payment you used to buy it. (Note: This is built on the assumption that from the day you receive a distribution from a retirement account, you typically have around 60 days to return the funds into your account to avoid paying a penalty (typically about 10%) plus income tax on the amount you took as an early distribution if you're under the age of 59 1/2.)

Here's how it would work: from retirement account number one, take a distribution for the 20% down payment you need to become the owner of a single-family home. Before 60 days pass, take a distribution from retirement account number two to pay yourself back what you borrowed from retirement account number one. Sixty days later, because you've been saving for your down payment, pay yourself back into account number two to avoid the penalties. Congratulations! You've just paid zero percent interest on your down payment and paid your retirement accounts back in full.

The IRS typically allows you to borrow and repay yourself once every 12 months. You can get creative loaning money to yourself (and your spouse) this way: borrowing and repaying between retirement accounts, returning funds within 60 days. Chat with your tax professionals and your plan custodians on the specifics related to your account type to understand the potential tax consequences of taking early distributions, just in case you don't pay yourself back in the required time.

Borrowing from a bank

In these times of mergers and consolidations, when local banks are swallowed up by national corporations, it's harder than ever to qualify for a bank loan. Even if the local branch manager is your tennis buddy, chances are your loan application will be sent to a loan service center in another state. It will be processed by a computer that cares about only three things: your social security number, your annual income, and your credit rating.

If you have a high annual income and good credit rating, the computer might spit out a favorable answer. Otherwise, you're just

plain out of luck. Computers don't care about extenuating factors, such as your trustworthiness, your willingness to give up vacations for the next five years, or the fact that your grandmother is rich and one day you'll inherit her fortune. Typically, the bank manager can't override the decision of the ultimate number-cruncher.

The old adage is true now more than ever: banks only lend money to those who don't need it.

Is there a way to get around this? Yes and no. If it means playing a kind of round-robin game by opening as many credit lines in as many banks as possible, then no. File that idea under hare-brained scheme (and that may be an injustice to rabbit intelligence.) Unless you're a financial wizard, playing games with banks and multiple lines of credit is a sure way to mess up your credit rating.

Maybe you've noticed that banks are not very playful. It's better to approach them as you would an unfriendly giant that you hope to recruit as a player for your basketball team. You've got to woo him a little and offer him his favorite food—in this case, your money.

Having a relationship with your bank staff is the best way to establish yourself as a worthy loan applicant. By relationship, I don't mean dinners and flowers. I mean, keeping all your accounts in the same place and getting to know the bank manager and loan officers. If you feel like small potatoes at your current bank, look for a smaller, more local operation (like a credit union or community bank) that may be more appreciative of your business. Every time you need a loan, be it a home equity loan, car loan, or business loan, look to your bank for financing. After paying back a few secured loans on time, they'll get to know you as a safe credit risk. In the world of banking relationships, that's as good as being engaged.

Borrowing from credit cards (beware!!!)

Borrowing money from credit cards is an option, but not one I recommend. Credit card money is probably the most expensive money you can borrow. Credit cards charge high interest—and the interest you pay is not tax deductible.

Before you take cash advances from your credit cards, consider whether another way to borrow is available to you. Any one of the other possibilities outlined above is better for your financial fitness.

If borrowing from credit cards is the only way for you to raise a down payment for your first investment home, be certain that you meet the following criteria:

- You have excellent credit, and you plan to keep it that way.
- You have very little outstanding debt.
- You can afford the extra payments.
- You're responsible. Very responsible.

In other words, be sure you have enough income and enough discipline to pay off the amount drawn from your credit cards within a few months. If you allow credit card balances to remain much longer than that, you're going to pay a very steep price. Above all, be aware of the true cost involved before you borrow from credit cards.

Partner with a friend who is cash-rich but time-poor

Here's an additional capital-access method that may be available to some people: find yourself a partner who is cash-rich but time-poor. Find a partner who will be happy to have you take the lead in learning and doing the investing (with support from our infrastructure team) while she/he provides the capital to invest. Typically, your partner will get all their money back upon the future sale or refi of the property. You might also propose a 50/50 or 60/40 or 70/30 split of equity gains and net income for some period of time or until the property is sold. Whatever you decide, please use a lawyer to prepare a contract outlining all terms, roles, responsibilities, timelines, contingencies, etc.

Buying properties as an entity that is not you: the self-directed IRA

Do you have traditional or Roth IRA retirement accounts you may have forgotten to look at for several years? Are those funds invested heavily in stocks and bonds, and perhaps you'd like to diversify with a few single-family home investments? Maybe the IRA funds are invested in a way that they aren't growing much at all?

Another technique I've seen people use to buy their single-family home rentals is buying properties within a self-directed IRA. If you don't currently have at least $60,000 to $80,000 in a traditional or Roth IRA retirement account, you can either skip this section or read it out of curiosity.

How does this work? First, if you already have a self-directed IRA, call your custodian and ask if they allow single-family home rental investments within the IRA. You may find out your institution doesn't allow this asset type to be purchased with IRA funds. If that's the case, work with a specialized custodian to set up a new self-directed IRA for this purpose and initiate an asset transfer.

This technique lets you buy rental homes from inside your IRA account. Well, it's not really *you* that is buying the rental home; it's your IRA that's buying. When you use a self-directed IRA to buy rental homes, you can use cash in the account for your down payment or to buy the home outright. You can also get specialized loans within the IRA to finance the purchase. These are called non-recourse loans and are not the usual loans you get in the open market. These loans are offered by special lenders who have certain requirements. This is a secured loan backed by collateral (usually the property being purchased). However, as a non-recourse loan, the only security the lender will have access to will be the home purchased. The lender cannot go after the IRA account in case there is a deficiency.

To buy a home with a non-recourse loan made to your self-directed IRA, you'll need a bigger down payment. 30–40% is typical. I suggest learning the important details like the tax implications, if any, before using this entity. (And, yes, we cover this at our ICG events, and we bring in experts to speak about it, if you are interested in learning more.)

If you choose to partner with a family member or a cash-rich but time-poor friend for your 20% down payment, you may be so excited to get started that you consider skipping the written document and moving forward with verbal agreements. Whatever you do—do not fall into this trap! It is absolutely worth the time to get this done. And, once you've got your partner lined up, we will be happy to connect you to an attorney to draft the agreement that will help you both begin this exciting journey.

INVESTOR STORY
In His Own Words

I understand that some people may find the idea of borrowing money from friends or family a bit uncomfortable. Let me share a story of an ICG investor...an inspiring tale that will likely make more people think about using that option if no other is available. Borrowing your down payment from a friend or family member is a good way to begin to build your own solid financial future. The investor you're about to meet used not one but *two* of the cash-access tips in this chapter to buy his first three properties. This interview with him took place in 2018.

Peter worked in the computer services industry. He shared that he always preferred to stay in the ranks of the technical people, shying away from managerial positions because, as he says it, "I find people more difficult than machines."

"In 1992, in my early fifties, I finally decided it was time to buy my own place after renting for decades," shares Peter. "I wanted to buy a studio apartment that was in foreclosure in NYC as my primary residence. A 20% down payment of the $45,000 price was required, but I did not have $9000 in cash."

Not feeling like being deterred, he approached a friend who was in a position to help.

"I borrowed the down payment from friends and paid the informal loan back a little bit each month," Peter said. "I was very responsible about paying my friends back. I did what I needed to do to buy that first place, but you know what? Buying my first home gave me a new state of mind that maybe I can do this. I was born in Romania and came here as a not-so-young man. I wasn't a confident person."

Several years later, after turning sixty, Peter began to think about his future.

> "I was past 60. I had no savings, and I had a lot of debt. I had spent my money like a drunken sailor. Growing up in Eastern Europe, I didn't know about things like saving or investing for someday. I was living in the moment. Suddenly, I realized I had a problem. If I continued like this, I would have the freedom to sleep under any bridge I wished. I knew I had to do something, to invest in something, but I did not have any savings. I had nothing. I was in a profound panic. And so, in the early months of the year 2000, I went to hear Adiel speak at the Learning Annex in New York City."

At that event, when I first met Peter, as I've done in this book, I explained where and what to buy.

> "Adiel suggested we buy new homes. At the time he was buying in Arizona and Florida," recalled Peter. "Then Adiel mentioned Oviedo, Florida, twenty minutes north of Orlando. I had been there many times because my lady's son lived there. How lucky I felt! When Adiel mentioned Phoenix, I realized I knew that city too. I had done a consulting job there. So suddenly it didn't feel so scary to me. Within a month of hearing Adiel speak, I looked at a home being built in Oviedo. I was asked for $1000 earnest money deposit. I didn't have it. I did have overdraft protection, though, so I wrote the check. I closed on that house in August of 2000."

While I don't recommend you write checks because you have overdraft protection, I'm sharing that Peter did that because he did not want to miss his opportunity to buy his first single-family home rental. It worked for him and he secured the contract. But what about the down payment he needed a few months later to buy that home in Florida?

> "I paid the loan off for my New York City studio in eight years. In that time, it had appreciated in value enough to secure a $25,000 home equity line of credit (HELOC). I used that money to raise

the down payment to buy my first properties. Remember, having turned sixty, I felt it was do or die time for me."

After buying his first rental home in Oviedo, Florida, Peter got even *more* serious about taking action to build for his future. Within two months of attending my talk in New York, Peter bought a second rental home, this time in Phoenix, Arizona.

"To buy that second property, as I did for my first rental home purchase in Florida, I entered into an 80/10/10 arrangement (80% first mortgage, 10% second mortgage and 10% down.) I fondly remember Patricia, one of the ICG realtors in Phoenix. She was fantastic and very helpful to me. I closed on that home in Phoenix just two months after buying in Florida."

At this point, Peter paused to emphasize something he wants potential investors to consider *if* they decide to borrow from friends or family members to get started.

"Every time I borrowed, whether from a friend or from a bank, I did it responsibly," he stated. "While I didn't have a formal payback plan when I borrowed from my friends, I never borrowed over my head. I always had a vision of being able to service my debts in a timely manner. I had a well-paying IT job, and I worked hard to pay off my loans."

Peter is about to celebrate turning 80. He owns six homes, four of which he purchased as an ICG investor. He held on to the home he bought in Phoenix, two homes in two cities in Texas and one in West Palm Beach, Florida. He sold the first home he purchased in Oviedo and used those gains to buy additional properties.

Let's pause to really appreciate Peter's story. Can you imagine how different Peter's life would be today if he hadn't bought his first property (the studio) years before? What if he never purchased that first asset that created the equity he eventually accessed as a $25,000 HELOC to buy rental homes? What if Peter had been too shy to ask a friend to loan him the down payment back then? Where would he be now?

When I asked Peter how he feels about his experiences, his net worth, and his financial future, he really opened up.

> "To answer this question is a confession," he reveals. "Some folks have confidence in their ability and their trade. I didn't trust myself to be able to 'make it.' At age 60, I had zero hope for the future and felt I was at a dead end. Investing in single-family homes has saved my life. Had I not done this, I would be living in poverty now. Instead, I'm asset rich and have enough income to support my needs as I prepare to turn 80—and for years to come. I have enough equity to worry about nothing. I owe my peace of mind all to one man: Adiel Gorel. I have enormous respect for him."

Hearing these heartfelt words from people who have applied the advice I've been giving for over thirty years, people whose lives have literally been transformed for the better, is the greatest reward for me. It's why I speak, write, and share my experiences and knowledge.

I want there to be *more* stories that turn out like Peter's story, when the investor begins at age 60 because he or she knows it's not too late. I want there to be *less* stories like what could've happened to Peter had he not taken the actions he did.

Peter has some advice for people who are still *thinking* about buying.

"The best day to buy is always today," he says. "Go ahead and do it. You'll have seven million reasons why not to do it—none of those reasons count. I had a real can-do attitude when I started, believing that if there's a will, there is a way. Find it! Not having the cash today is just another reason for not doing what you should do. The sooner you do it, the better off you'll be. It's a wonderful thing."

He concludes with, "Whatever you do, don't buy the cheap houses. That's likely to be a management-intensive experience. Listen to Adiel's advice about where and what to buy. Above all, don't doubt yourself. I'm living proof that it can be done."*—Peter, ICG investor for 19 years. Owns six single-family homes in Florida, Arizona, Texas, and elsewhere*

REPLAY

- **There are many ways you can access the cash you need for the down payment for your first single-family home investment. Among these methods are earning it, saving it, borrowing it or partnering with someone who is cash-rich but time-poor.**

- **The best day to buy is always today. The sooner you do it, the better off you'll be.**

CHAPTER 6

Breaking the Ice — The Process of Buying Your First Single-Family Home Rental

So far, you've come to appreciate why you need a financial plan for the long term. You understand that whatever investments you assemble for your future must be able to beat the inflation we know exists. You've seen that investing in single-family homes is one of the best things you can do for your financial future. You've come to appreciate the magic of the 30-year fixed-rate loan like never before. And you've learned best practices regarding where, what, and why to buy. Now let's get you ready to purchase your first single-family home rental. Let's help you break the ice.

Buying your first investment home is the biggest hurdle. After all, you're traveling in uncharted territory—the new world of investing in single-family homes. No doubt you'll have many questions (and perhaps a few fears). But as you go through the process of buying your first investment home, your questions will be answered, and your fears put to rest. I've found something else happens when you take this step: an increased confidence and sense of empowerment that comes from taking control of your financial future.

In this chapter, I'm first going to encourage you to take stock of your finances and outline what I believe you should have in place before purchasing your first investment property. Then I'll take you through the process of breaking the ice: the steps you'll experience (the steps thousands have already taken), as you prepare to buy that first single-family home.

The most important property you will buy is that first one. Let me also say this right away: you should plan to buy more than one home, so you can have multiple data points. If you bought one single-family home and it rented in one day, which isn't very common, you learned something, but you haven't learned very much. If you buy a second home, and it takes two and a half months to rent, which also isn't very common, now you have two data points. When you acquire your third single-family home to rent, now you'll have three data points. At that point, you'll start to see what an average experience looks like. Also, by the time you buy your third rental property, you'll find the whole process to be much easier. And of course, you don't have to move fast to acquire multiple properties; you can go at whatever pace works best for your financial plan.

So, the first goal to focus on now is to buy single-family home number one. To do that, first give yourself a financial health checkup.

Assess your financial health before you begin

Financial fitness is the basis of sound financial planning. By "financially fit," I don't mean wealthy. What I mean instead is that you have a solid understanding of your overall financial picture and a feasible budget that includes funds for investing. Becoming financially fit means knowing where you need to go and how you'll get there.

Before you begin investing, it's a good idea to take a careful look at the big picture. Assess what you own, what you owe, and how much cash and credit are available to you. To do this, you'll need to calculate your net worth and analyze your expenditures. Your annual income,

the amount of debt you carry, your spending habits, and your attitude about money will all play a part in the way you invest and how you structure your financial plan.

Your net worth: Net worth is the wealth you've accumulated to date—the amount that's left over after subtracting your liabilities from your assets. *Assets* include cash and savings, your home and personal property, stocks and bonds, real estate, privately owned businesses, and retirement accounts. *Liabilities* include mortgage(s), car loans or leases, student or other loans, and credit card debt.

Your net worth is your financial barometer. It reveals the reserves you have to tap into—or the opposite—how your liabilities may be undermining your assets. The worksheet that follows will help you see this big picture quite clearly.

Once you've calculated your net worth, you will see at a glance how your assets and liabilities stack up. While there's no hard-and-fast rule about how much you should have, or the percentage of liabilities to assets, you may discover some surprises. Perhaps your credit card debt has just about wiped out the positive figures in the assets section. Or perhaps your home equity, stocks, or retirement accounts have grown more than you anticipated. Your net worth statement shows how your assets and debts are distributed. When it comes time to raise cash or apply for a loan, this information will be very helpful to you, so please make this your first step.

NET WORTH WORKSHEET

ASSETS	
CASH AND SAVINGS	$
INVESTMENTS	
STOCKS & MUTUAL FUNDS	
BONDS & BOND MUTUAL FUNDS	
STOCK OPTIONS	
VALUE OF PRIVATELY OWNED BUSINESS	
INVESTMENT REAL ESTATE	
CASH VALUE OF LIFE INSURANCE POLICIES	
OTHER INVESTMENTS	
TOTAL INVESTMENTS	$
RETIREMENT ACCOUNTS	
IRAs	
401(k), 401(b)	
SELF-EMPLOYED PLANS (Keogh, etc.)	
ANNUITIES	
EST. VALUE OF COMPANY PENSION	
TOTAL RETIREMENT ACCOUNTS	$
HOME & PERSONAL PROPERTY	
HOME	
VACATION HOME	
CARS, RECREATIONAL VEHICLES	
ART, COLLECTIBLES, JEWELRY, FURNISHINGS	
OTHER PERSONAL ASSETS	
TOTAL HOME & PERSONAL PROPERTY	$
TOTAL ASSETS	$
LIABILITIES	
MORTGAGE DEBT	
CAR LOANS/LEASE	
STUDENT LOANS	
CREDIT CARD BALANCES	
OTHER LOANS	
OTHER DEBT	
TOTAL LIABILITIES	$
NET WORTH (subtract liabilities from assets)	$

PAUSE

It's important to update your net worth statement on a regular basis, typically once a year. It's a good way to keep in touch with your financial goals, and make sure you're on the right path. Watching your net worth increase will help you stay focused and keep your enthusiasm high. Long-term investing requires discipline, and sometimes it can feel as if the rewards don't come soon enough. Your net worth statement transforms the abstract into black and white—you'll see the results of your hard work on the bottom line.

Protecting your assets: Another component of your financial fitness is ensuring you and your assets are protected. Comprehensive insurance coverage is your primary defense against unforeseen—and potentially disastrous—events. It's true that insurance premiums take a bite out of your budget and may seem at times like unnecessary expenses. Without proper insurance, however, you're gambling with your future, and with what you've worked so hard to achieve.

There are four major areas of your life that need to be insured against loss: yourself, your dependents, your potential earnings, and your property. In my book *Remote Control Retirement Riches,* I explain these four types of insurance (health insurance, life insurance, disability insurance, property insurance) and why they matter. All are important components to have in place before you begin investing in single-family homes.

Here I only want to emphasize one point about the last type: homes, cars, and other property should be insured for their replacement cost. In addition, liability coverage protects you against lawsuits. Homeowners and auto insurance generally include some amount of liability coverage; check your records or call your property insurance agent to make sure it's an adequate amount. You may also want to look into buying an umbrella insurance policy, also known as excess liability insurance. A good rule of thumb is to insure yourself for at least twice the amount of your net worth. This is another reason to update your net worth worksheet annually.

Now that you've assessed your financial big picture, let's talk about what you'll need to start.

How much money you'll need to get started

Although some insist you can purchase real estate with "no money down," the truth is most real estate investments require an initial outlay of cash.

Exactly how much cash depends, of course, on the price of the property, the amount of leverage you use, and the associated closing costs. To keep it simple, though, I suggest you set a goal of approximately $50,000.

Why $50,000? Because it's about enough to cover a 20% down payment and closing costs on a property priced at $200,000. This amount is the low/average price of a quality single-family home in the markets I've recommended. As of this writing, there exists the possibility of choosing a down payment of only 15% down, which would make the sum needed about $40,000. However, we will use $50,000 in our example.

One important point as we talk about getting started: if all the cash you have in the world is the money you intend to use as a down payment, please don't pursue this investment. Why? Because you *must* have cash reserves as a property owner. You must be prepared for unexpected situations that may arise. Buying an investment property with all the cash you have is not something I ever recommend. At least not yet. That's why I emphasized the net worth worksheet as the first step—to understand what you currently have.

If you don't have the $50,000 (plus reserves) available to invest just yet, we have explored several ways to raise capital in the previous chapter. In this chapter, I want to next take you through the steps that will help you break the ice. I will describe the process of purchasing your first single-family home, what to expect, and how it feels to do it as part of a proven ecosystem that's helped thousands of people before you.

Remember that this $50,000 will become the cornerstone of your financial future. Immediately after you get your home rented, the process starts: Your 30-year fixed-rate loan starts getting eroded as your tenant pays your mortgage, and inflation does its thing. Your home equity value also starts the typical, gradual increase you'll enjoy over the long term (despite occasional booms and busts), and so on.

Your financial future will be so much stronger because you made this 20% down payment on your first single-family home.

For now, let's say you have access to $50,000—in a savings account, money market fund, or elsewhere. You're ready to invest—now what? If you're very busy, looking for the right property (in the right market, using the right realtor, the right lender, the right property manager, etc.) may simply be too time-consuming. Happily, that's exactly where my experience and the infrastructure I've built come in.

The single-family home investment process

Let's compare the experiences in the previous chapter (the apartment owner in Santa Cruz who had to sell her Seacliff home and the couple who invested in Detroit sight unseen) to what your experience can be like when you choose to buy your first single-family home with a proven infrastructure behind you.

ICG facilitates the ecosystem we have built, which has helped thousands of investors build wealth for over 30 years. Working with a group of industry professionals and fellow investors like ICG may mean the difference between investing and not investing. If you have little time to look for properties and assess markets far from home,

I suggest you attend an ICG Expo soon to see how we coordinate real estate investments for private investors.

You'll see how the ecosystem has done the initial legwork for you, assessing Sun Belt state markets, upcoming developments, and specific properties available for purchase. You'll notice right away that we've created a type of support system that can help you throughout the life of your investment. When you invest through our ecosystem, you benefit from being part of a large group of investors who have influence with realtors and property managers.

Of course, I always strongly recommend that you visit the market, see the homes, and meet both the brokers in the field and the property managers. Ultimately, it is you who decides whether to invest or not. However, following in the footsteps of others does make it easier.

Our realtors keep an eye out for newly permitted neighborhoods. They meet with builders and call to inform us of new opportunities. We then notify potential investors in our community who are looking to buy.

When you attend an ICG Expo, you will first notice that right there in front of you are various real estate brokers. They all come from Sun Belt markets we've analyzed and selected as good places to invest in single-family homes. These real estate professionals bring a plethora of information about neighborhoods being developed and the communities in which they're located. You will see the planned developments and those currently under construction. You will see how many homes are planned for each neighborhood, which homes have already been reserved by other investors, and which ones are available for your consideration.

You can ask the expert market broker questions about the property managers they work with, the typical length of time it takes to rent the home once it's fully constructed, and so on.

The broker will show you the plans available for you to choose from, complete with full spec sheets (offers of the houses they have for sale).

These spec sheets should include most of the information you'll need to make a decision about the property's investment value: a photograph of the house, its location, size (number of bedrooms, bathrooms, square footage), price, and monthly rental rates (low-to-high range) in the area. Spec sheets also typically include the principal and interest payments based on 20%, 25% or 30% down payments (for example) and the different mortgages associated with those down payments. The spec sheet may also include information about annual property taxes and a basic cash flow analysis.

At a recent expo, we had real estate brokers in attendance from eight different markets. In just one day, potential investors were able to evaluate single-family homes in all those cities across the Sun Belt, representing at least a dozen different developments.

In 2021, due to the COVID pandemic, our expos are via Zoom, and we have shortened the duration to four hours. A silver lining to the Zoom format is that people can join from all over the world without having to travel.

Also in 2021, the demand for single-family homes is very high, and supply strains to keep up. As a result, you may find yourself on a waiting list, waiting for available properties. I personally don't mind waiting a few months on a waiting list. These are long-term investments, and a few months make little difference.

Prices have been going up in most markets due to the increased demand and low supply. However, the interest rates as of August 2021 (as I am writing this), are the lowest they have ever been. In addition, we have already experienced several months of higher inflation. Economists predict inflation getting higher in the coming months and years, due to the massive government infrastructure plans, which call for the printing of trillions of dollars. Getting a 30-year fixed-rate mortgage at the lowest rates ever, then heading into a period of higher inflation, is a dream come true for the savvy investor. Inflation will erode the true value of the fixed debt at a faster clip.

Let's say you decide you want to buy one of thosehomes. What happens next?

You express your desire to the real estate broker to reserve one of these new homes. Your name goes on the lot you have chosen (or better still, let the broker choose for you, since they are local and can evaluate which lot they like). Since builders typically offer at least two plans to choose from (4 bedrooms vs. 3 bedrooms, for example), the broker may ask you to choose which plan you want for your first single-family home rental. Then you simply provide your contact information. Within a couple of weeks, you will receive a contract from the builder to purchase this home. At that point, you'll be asked to put down an earnest money deposit of about $2,000 or more, depending on the market and the builder.

Of course, by this point, I hope (especially as a new buyer), you will already have visited the market and have a feel for the area. While attending and learning at our ICG Expo is a great thing to do, it should not replace visiting the market in person.

Usually, it is about four to eight months from the time you hear about the new homes at one of our Expos and the time your rental home is completed, but the timeline can be delayed due to weather, approvals, etc. Most builders try to have homes available to occupy in the summer, since that is when most families choose to move.

Homes will also be shown to you outside of our expos. As people get in touch with us, which usually ends up in a phone call with me, we connect them to the lead brokers in our markets. From then on, they work directly with the local broker team in that market. ICG, and me specifically, are always available for support, questions, issues, and planning. During 2021, home construction may take longer than normal due to supply chain delays, building materials shortages, and labor shortages. To me, a longer time to build the homes makes no difference. These are long-term investments.

After you reserve your future rental home, you can start making plans to get your financing together. You can plan to apply for a 30-year

fixed-rate loan and to access funds for your 20% down payment. You can decide to work with a lender you already know can initiate loans in the state where you want to buy, or you can ask us to introduce you to the broker with a proven track record with whom we work. In 2021, many builders prefer that the buyer work with a lender who had already proven they can close loans successfully in their state.

In *Remote Control Retirement Riches*, I dedicated an entire section to financing, evaluating different mortgages, the importance of good credit, etc. In this book, I'm focused on sharing expertise specifically to help you buy your first single-family home rental. For starters, allow me to make one point about closing costs that I often hear from those making their first purchase.

In your loan paperwork, you will see various closing costs. Some of these aren't really closing costs—think of them as "prepaids." These line items include insurance and property tax, so in essence, it's still your money—these are not loan expenses paid to a third party. If these weren't being collected when your new loan closes, as it is basically a standard procedure, you would be paying insurance and property tax anyway in a few months. It's just collected in advance and held in an escrow account for you by your lender. Why? They don't want to take the chance that you won't make these important payments; remember the lender has a much greater stake in the property than you do at the very beginning.

So now that you've lined up your financing and your broker has told you when the house will be completed, you can get ready to close the transaction. As I said before, it is also a good idea to visit the market before you decide which home to buy, so as to understand the market better and make a more informed decision. Go there to visit the broker, see the neighborhood, and experience your investment for yourself. While there, I suggest you take the advice of the broker regarding the options you'll be asked to decide for the house, with an eye toward choosing elements that will be most appealing to your future tenants. Making these choices while the home is under construction is one of the benefits of buying a brand-new home. However, I would defer to the local broker and property manager in choosing everything, since they know what works well with local tenants.

Investing in a brand-new home

Buying a brand-new home—or one that's about to be built—offers a number of nifty advantages for investors.

The first is, of course, the house is new, and everything is (or should be) in near-perfect condition. If there are any flaws, they'll be repaired under the homebuilder's warranty. You won't have to worry about repairs and refurbishments for at least the first few years. There's no need to paint or put in new carpet. For busy investors, new homes are a godsend.

The second is that, because you're buying the house knowing it will be a rental property, you can select the floor coverings, finishes, and appliances that will work best in a rental home. You'll want to choose neutral colors, durable (but not pricey) floor coverings, and appliances that can withstand the wear and tear of tenant turnover. Keeping an eye toward utility, not cosmetic beauty, will keep your initial expenses down and minimize future replacement costs. Your local broker can provide invaluable advice about these choices.

You can also choose a low-maintenance landscaping style. In some hot Sun Belt areas, this often means using drought-resistant plants and a drip system. Tenants aren't always avid gardeners, and a low-maintenance yard will reduce the need for a landscaping service, while keeping the yard attractive. In other states, the common landscaping might be a lawn in the front. Go with what is common and normally expected in the local marketplace.

A third bonus is you can negotiate with builders for added amenities. We usually give builders a significant volume of sales when our investors and I buy through our local brokers, making everyone a "large client" (even if they just bought one home). This, in some cases, allows our local brokers to eke out extra benefits for our investors. Sometimes the prices of new homes are fixed, but builders are willing to offer upgrades such as a tile entry or backyard landscaping at no extra cost. In a tight market where the builders sell well, these incentives may be less common.

Because you are working within our established infrastructure, you can certainly ask other investors who have single-family homes under property management to recommend a management company to you. We certainly do that (as does our local broker). When you're in the market conducting your assessment, or visiting the home under construction, it's a fantastic idea to meet with the property management team used by our other investors, as you will have "ICG Clout." The local broker will arrange the meeting. Talk to the manager, ask questions, and understand the rental market. This is part of your education.

Now what? Take a deep breath. You've selected your first single-family home investment and arranged for your financing through a 30-year fixed-rate loan. You have your 20% down payment available. You've visited the Sun Belt community where your investment is located. You've met your broker and made decisions about amenities

that will go into your future rental home. You've met with the property management team. You've *almost* broken the ice! What's left? Once you close on your first single-family home and it's rented; the ice will have been broken.

In the next chapter, you'll begin your basic training as an investor. I'll show you how it works after this single-family home is yours.

ECOSYSTEM BENEFIT
Guidance on Where and What to Buy When Choosing Single-Family Home Rentals

Jon and Irene are a married couple in Northern California who began investing in single-family homes with ICG in 2016 at the age of 40. Before that, they had purchased rental homes in California, Nevada, and Texas. They knew that real estate markets were rebounding at that time and needed to find properties that weren't overpriced. So, they attended an ICG Expo and made their move.

When asked about the benefits of working within our infrastructure to buy that first single-family home, Jon said, "If you're brand new and trying to get your foot in the door, get with a group like ICG. Work with someone with experience who can mentor you through the first investment. The first time you're doing anything is the hardest. Please believe it gets easier. You won't appreciate all of this until you do it. So go ahead...jump in the pool. There IS a lifeguard!"

Jon also shared something typical of investors in the ICG community. They like to share information and experiences. "Last week we were at a party with friends. They hadn't seriously considered real estate as an investment for their retirement. I told my friends that I'm willing to share information with them about how we're doing this so they're not going at it alone." I hope they come to an ICG Expo soon.

Jon said he and Irene are very "grateful for the experiences and the investment opportunities that have been presented to us so far. We're thankful that we got connected to this group and we will certainly grow with this group. It's a relationship that we will continue to foster. I hope Adiel never retires. He's a good guy."

INVESTOR STORY
In Their Own Words

Jon and Irene, the married couple introduced above, had invested in the stock market for 12 years before considering investing in single-family homes. Jon was on a professional track to be a scientist. A sudden layoff caused them to seriously consider building their own secure financial future.

> They began investing in rental homes because as Jon said, "Savvy investors know to invest both in tangible assets like real estate and also in the stock market for the long-term."

Since attending the first ICG Expo, they have purchased three homes in Florida and three homes in Oklahoma.

Jon said, "We feel good and are continuing to grow our portfolio. We are happy that we started! My advice is this: the best way to learn and grow is to take action."— *Jon and Irene have been investing with ICG for two years. They now own eight single-family homes at the age of 42. They're well on their way to building a portfolio that will provide long-term benefits.*

REPLAY

- Buying one single-family home should be your first goal.
- Becoming financially fit means understanding your overall financial picture and setting goals.
- Comprehensive insurance coverage is your primary defense against unforeseen events.
- Contribute to at least one retirement plan.
- The $50,000 you sow today will likely reap over $350,000 in 20 years.
- Set up a separate account for investment funds.
- A "spec sheet" should include:
- Exterior photograph and address of property
- Style, age, size, and price of property
- List of important features and upgrades
- Breakdown of monthly income and expenses
- Estimate of monthly cash flow

CHAPTER 7

Basic Training and Beyond: You've Purchased Your First Rental Home — Now What?

Congratulations. You made the decision to buy your single-family home rental. You've almost broken the ice. Now it's time for your basic training.

Let's talk about the closing process, getting your home rented, and what it feels like after that.

After you chose the home, you received a contract. It likely included an earnest money deposit clause. In the $200,000 price range, for which we'll estimate you'll need about $50,000 to close this transaction (20% down plus all loan closing costs, etc.), this initial earnest money deposit is typically about $2000 to $3000 in many markets. In some markets, especially in some areas in Florida, the initial deposit may be higher (sometimes quite a bit higher). This deposit goes into the escrow account at the title company (think of it like a third-party insurance company). There are some exceptions for some Florida vacation home communities. In other countries, it is common for a buyer and seller to each have their own lawyer and the lawyers get together to create the transaction. In most states in the U.S., the closing process is usually done by a title company that fills both of those roles and does so as a neutral third party.

The title company maintains an escrow account to collect all monies related to the transaction. They check the county records to verify that the seller really owns the home. They see if there are any liens on the home. If there are liens, the transaction cannot go forward until the seller clears them all. At the end of the transaction, the title company will issue title insurance for the buyer. This is something also unique to the U.S.

Buyers outside the U.S. especially appreciate the role of title companies. Not only will the deed be recorded in your name in the county records once the home is yours, but also if there's any issue with the deed (or a lien later surfaces that was missed) it should not be your responsibility. It's legally the title company's responsibility because they issued your title insurance. The premium for this title insurance is included in the closing costs. It appears as part of the final costs of the transaction.

If the property is ready to close, all that's left to do is finalize your financing. Once your loan is approved, closing can happen. For this to happen, typically the title company will send you the closing documents by email. A couple of documents will need to be notarized, but most can be simply printed and signed. One of these documents (which does *not* need to be notarized) is called a Settlement Statement (HUD1). It's a convenient line-by-line form that makes it easy to get your questions answered by the title company officer as you're going through the closing process.

An important tip for the first-time buyer: all the calculations—the first prorated mortgage payment and the majority of numbers on

the settlement statement—are based on the target closing date. It's very, very important that when you receive the package, you're very responsive about getting everything notarized, signed, and returned. Any delays that affect the closing date can be costly, so plan to be responsive to the title company in order to close on time. The title company usually sends you a FedEx or UPS prepaid label to ship the signed documents back—simple.

Once you ship the package, you're almost done.

The title company now has all the documents required to close on the buyer's side of the agreement (that's you). At this point, they will send you instructions to wire the rest of the funds needed for closing. If you put down $2000 earnest money, you'll need to wire the remaining approximately $48,000 (in this example of a $200,000 property) to the escrow account of the title company. Now the title company has your documents, your down payment, and all funds for the closing costs.

When your transaction is ready to close, your lender will fund your loan. This just means your lender will wire the entire loan amount you've borrowed to the escrow account at the title company. Now the title company has everything needed from you to close the buyer's side of the agreement.

At the same time, the title company has sent closing documents to the seller to sign and notarize, including the deed to the property. Note: If you're located outside the United States, you'll need to make an appointment at the American Embassy to find a notary for all paperwork that requires American notarization; some title companies also accept non-U.S. Embassy notaries under certain restrictions.

The title company now has everything they need to close the transaction. They go to the county records office and record the notarized documents, including the deed that makes you the owner of the home. It also records the deed of trust or mortgage regarding the bank's security of the loan. The title company then pays the funds to the seller for their property. At this point, the home is now yours. Congratulations!

About two or three weeks before that closing happens, the property management company you've been referred to (via the local broker that is part of our ecosystem) will contact you. They will have been alerted by the broker that you will be closing soon. They'll send their standard property management agreement. You simply review it, ask any questions you may have, sign, and return it. This agreement gives your property manager the right to represent you in the marketplace, to find a tenant, and to take care of the rental home for you.

Typically, before the closing, the broker will also arrange for insurance to be purchased via a local insurance agent. You're invited to talk to the agent so as to understand how to choose the coverage appropriate for your rental home. The insurance premium is usually paid for at closing.

Now you have insurance, you have hired a professional property manager, and the home is yours.

Basic training

If this is your first time buying a rental home, I call this period— the moment the home closed and became yours—"basic training."

At this point, I sometimes hear fear and uncertainty in the voices of many first-time investors, which is understandable, especially for those who have never purchased *any* home before. So, let me address a couple of common questions I get about what happens after the home is yours.

I'm often asked by beginning buyers: *What if my rental home doesn't rent?*

When you buy in large metropolitan areas with the criteria we've described earlier in this book, there's usually no such thing as a property that doesn't rent. There are only properties where rent is initially too high. The solution is to lower the advertised rent amount gradually until the single-family home rents. In 2021, the average vacancy rate in our Sun Belt markets is under 3%. You'll see: Soon after breaking the ice by buying home number one, that single-family homes do indeed rent.

Let me ask you a question about the neighborhood where you live. You may be living anywhere in the U.S. or in another country. You know the street on which you live. Let's say I want to buy a house on your street. You know your street extremely well. But I am very nervous because I'm in Northern California in the San Francisco Bay Area. I don't know your street, your town, your city...or perhaps I don't even know your country.

So, I ask you "What if I buy a house on your street and it never rents, or what if it doesn't rent for five years?"

You respond with, "Look, I live here on this street. That house will rent in one month!"

That's your experience. It's the same way property managers *know* their markets intimately. It's why they feel confident telling you that your single-family home *will* rent and at what monthly rent amount.

To help you get some of that confidence, I recommend you go in person to the community where you're thinking of buying. Visit with the property managers that other ICG investors have hired. Then, once you start buying your own properties, you'll feel much more comfortable having gained first-hand experience knowing your rental homes will rent.

Let's say it's been three weeks, and the home hasn't rented yet. You're nervous, you toss, and you turn. You know there's a mortgage payment coming due (remember mortgage payments are made in arrears and therefore, on average, the first mortgage payment is due about a month and a half after the closing—see below). Your inner voice drones on, saying things like:

"What have I done?"

"This is never going to rent."

"I knew it was too good to be true."

Then the property rents.

That is basic training.

I can tell you all about it, but I likely can't eliminate that stress for you completely the first time around. All I can do is let you know it may happen, and it is normal.

The average time to rent a home after closing in most of our markets in 2021 is about 45 days. [Actually, due to the high demand for single-family home rentals during the pandemic, we are seeing an average time that is closer to thirty days. However, I still prefer to be conservative and use an estimate of 45 days.] But your single-family home might take a week to rent, a day to rent, or two and a half months to rent. Whatever length of time it turns out to be, this is part of your basic training.

Once it rents, the process starts running, and then it actually becomes boring. That's how you know your basic training is over. By the way, basic training (thankfully) happens only when you purchase your first home.

The time between closing and the first mortgage payment

Let's talk about timing. If you have a mortgage, payments are made in arrears. Your May 1st payment is for the full month of April. Let's say you close on April 20th. At closing, you've already prepaid for April (a pro-rated amount from the 20th of April till the end of April), so your next payment will be for May, but that's not due until June 1st. So, in this example, you'll see that you've got a full month and 10 days before your first mortgage payment is due.

By the way, let's say the home you bought closes escrow on the 5th of April instead, you still don't have to make the first payment to your lender until June 1st. The June 1st payment will pay the mortgage for the month of May (that's what is meant by "in arrears"); the April portion of the payment was paid at the closing. That's almost two months to get it rented via your property manager. This is good information to know when you're planning a closing date with the title company.

With knowledge of this elapsed time between the closing date and the first mortgage payment due date, you can see it's possible for your property manager to plan to advertise the available rental very soon after closing. In some cases, under certain circumstances, the manager may even start advertising before the actual closing date.

When you meet with your new property manager, ask these questions (along with any others you may have): Can I see the advertising plan you have developed? How far in advance will you begin to advertise? How long does it typically take for a house to rent in this market?

Let the pros manage it

In *Remote Control Retirement Riches*, I explain what property managers do in great detail. Here, for brevity, I'll say this: Just as your stock portfolio or 401(k) is managed by someone who is familiar with the stock market, property managers are asset managers. They typically have vast experience working with many property owners and many tenants; they can do much to promote the profitability of your property. They can also help you avoid the problems that sometimes accompany property ownership.

A full-service property management company has four coordinating functions: people (tenant screening); financial (rent collection and disbursement, accounting services); construction (maintenance and repair); and legal (lease agreements, eviction proceedings). They are responsible for renting and managing your property in all its aspects. In most cases, when you hire a property manager, your rental home will require only a little of your time via the occasional phone call or email. If you're busy, professional property management is a must.

Think about this: Once you close escrow on your first property a thousand miles from your home, do you really want the responsibility of finding your first tenant? Of course not. That's the first moment professional property managers prove their value to you: They will advertise the home to potential tenants using their well-developed marketing processes to reach the people looking for housing in your neighborhood. They will show your single-family home to potential tenants and do all tenant screening steps (including credit and background checks). They'll handle the lease negotiation for you and collect all rent payments from your tenants.

For all the services they provide, property management companies charge a percentage of the gross rent collected monthly, usually somewhere between 8% and 10% (most of the ones we use charge 8%). On a house that rents for $1400 a month, the property management fee would be $112 to $140 per month. Their fee is deducted before a check (or direct deposit) is issued monthly to the property owner.

I recommend you decide on a maximum dollar amount your property manager is authorized to spend to deal with smaller maintenance issues that may arise. Specify this amount in the contract so you're not getting a phone call if a doorbell needs to be replaced. Beyond that dollar amount, direct your property manager, in writing, that she or he must email or call you for approval when larger maintenance issues arise that exceed the predetermined maximum amount.

When repairs do become necessary, the property management company will keep you apprised of what's needed and will coordinate the repairs by contacting tenants to arrange times for vendors or repairmen to come by. Often property managers work with a select group of contractors with whom they've negotiated discount pricing, which could save you money.

So, unless you want to get a phone call at 2 a.m. because the four-year-old tenant in your single-family home flushed her toy down the toilet (which is now backing up), please plan to always hire a property manager for your rental homes. This becomes especially obvious if you've invested in a rental home far from where you live. Note: Even when investors own rental homes in the city where they live, many hire property managers. These busy people don't want to get those emergency maintenance calls. They understand the value of professionals managing their properties, and you will too.

In short, the primary benefit to using a property manager is that it saves you time. You don't have to be an active landlord. You don't have to make rookie investor mistakes that can be costly. You don't have to learn the many skills involved to successfully manage rental properties—if you just let the professionals do it.

What happens after the home is rented

After the home is rented, your basic training is complete. From that point on, you might be curious as to what investor activities you'll need to do going forward. Let me describe what it looks and feels like to be an investor with a rental property.

On a monthly basis, you'll receive a check from your property manager that you will deposit, or the manager will direct-deposit the funds to the account you have designated. When your mortgage payment is due, you'll pay your lender (you can arrange for this action to be taken automatically). This process typically will take around 30 minutes each month.

I recommend you set up a separate bank account to manage your single-family homes' income and expenses. You'll thank me for this tip every year around tax time.

Your property manager will typically prepare an end-of-year statement, so you can see all income and expenses for the year. It will be easier to match this report to your records if you've created a separate account for your rental home transactions. Get into the habit of tracking your single-family home investments with a standard Profit & Loss (P&L) statement used by businesses. Create a P&L for each property as you buy more homes in the future. That way, you will understand the income and expenses associated with your property. By creating a Balance Sheet periodically, you can also see your net worth building as the years go by.

A small but important task that may require your attention as the owner of single-family home rentals: If you're not paying your property taxes and insurance on top of your monthly principal and interest payment to your lender (commonly referred to as PITI, which stands for Principal, Interest, Taxes, Insurance), then once (or in some counties twice) a year you will need to take time to pay for insurance and property taxes. This is a minimal time commitment. Just be sure you schedule it, so it's done.

Trust that you'll get used to the processes and short time commitment required to manage your single-family home rental. After you buy rental home number two, it will all be a repetition of what you did to purchase and manage the details of your first home. Homes number three, four, five, six. and more will be downright boring for you, because by then, you'll be comfortable with what's required.

ECOSYSTEM BENEFIT
Easy Introduction to the Professionals Who Will Manage Your Single-Family Home

Being introduced to a trusted property manager directly by the broker is a powerful benefit ICG investors have long enjoyed. It's a benefit that's as valuable to the first-time investor as it is to the person with double-digit homes in their portfolio.

So, how do we select those trusted property managers? When first entering a Sun Belt market, we ask for referrals from people I know and professionals I've worked with who know property managers in that market. We do our own due diligence on the recommended property managers. We talk to investors for whom they are managing properties. Then, we put them through what I call the "acid test." We buy some homes and let the property managers manage them for us. If we like how they do things, we will begin to connect them to investors in our group. That's one reason people who have been buying rental homes through our infrastructure feel so well served by the property managers we recommend.

Here are a couple examples of what our investors say about this valuable ecosystem benefit:

> "When buying my first rental home in Florida, I wanted Adiel to be very hands-on as I went through the process. He recommended a broker with whom he had worked. After I bought the home, Adiel recommended a property manager he had personally hired to manage his own rental properties. He goes first into each market. Having been satisfied with those services, he passes along information about them to his newbie investors. I was green even though I had just turned 60. Thank goodness I didn't have to do property management selection myself. I had no expertise whatsoever."—**Peter, ICG investor for 19 years. Owns six single-family homes in Florida, Arizona, Texas, and elsewhere**

It is possible for something unusual to arise when you own a rental home. In that case, it's helpful to have a group of fellow investors and professionals to help you solve a problem, instead of handling it on your own. Theresa's story illustrates this perfectly.

> She said, "The first rental home I bought was in Oklahoma. The broker referred me to a property manager, but the home didn't rent for a while. Not knowing any better, I thought this was normal due to the holiday season, but I wasn't happy. I shared the situation with a fellow ICG investor. He suggested I talk to Adiel, who agreed that it

should not be taking so long to rent in that market. Adiel got involved and my home was rented in two weeks. The lesson I learned was this: don't wait too long to ask your broker and/or Adiel to intervene. I regret being so patient and that I waited so long. I am very happy now with my property manager. I'm also happy that I talked to Adiel."

Professional property managers have a finger on the pulse of a community and can provide valuable information to owners as market conditions ebb and flow. It's certainly beneficial to have ICG's ecosystem backing the investors if glitches happen.

INVESTOR STORY
In His Own Words

You know how earlier I said it's important to break the ice by buying your first single-family home? Do you remember in this chapter I referred to the period between buying and getting your first home rented as your basic training? Do you recall that I said that buying your second, third, fourth, and so on rental home would be downright boring because you'll be so accustomed to the process?

Let me introduce you to Michael, an investor in Silicon Valley. Michael graduated from his basic training and then got really inspired to keep going as an investor. I have a feeling that his story will motivate you to hurry up and buy your first single-family home. His uniquely ambitious story will make you eager to graduate from basic training too.

Michael began investing in single-family rental homes in his mid-thirties.

"I was attracted to investing in single-family homes because of my desire for diversification both in asset classes and in income streams," Michael explains. "It was mid-2012, and my stock portfolio had experienced three strong years following the big dip and recession. I thought it was the right time to move some

money away from the stock market and invest in other assets.
In addition, having worked in the healthcare industry,
I had witnessed sudden layoffs. I saw my colleagues' professional
paths turn unexpectedly. I realized job security is out the window
and the next job isn't always neatly lined up. There is so much
uncertainty, and sometimes financial insecurity. Therefore,
I was also looking to generate additional income streams,
beyond earning a paycheck."

Michael continues about why he chose this asset class.

"I was referred to Adiel by a friend in Seattle who was thinking
about investing in single-family homes," said Michael. "I found
the combination of cash flows from rental income, principal
repayment by tenants, and asset appreciation over time very
compelling in achieving my goal of diversification. I also liked
the great leverage of using the 30-year fixed-rate loan with a low
interest rate, paid over time."

On the topic of saving and the long-term view, Michael said this:

"So many people struggle with the concept of saving. I compare
paying down those 30-year fixed-rate loans to a forced saving
mechanism, one that doesn't require you to make a proactive
decision to save. It just happens almost autonomously and leads
to great wealth creation over the long term. With rental homes,
I could remove some of the volatility associated with stocks,
establish additional stable income streams, and chart a consistent
path forward."

Michael also observed the benefit of using professional property
management companies.

"I saw that by hiring professional property management
companies, I could indeed scale up my investing," Michael
stated. "To further meet my goal of diversification within the
asset class of single-family homes, I've also been able to diversify
geographically by investing in different areas of the U.S."

Michael was interviewed just after his 42nd birthday, after he had closed on his 42nd rental home. Michael mentioned he had contracts to buy four more single-family homes this year.

> "I have set a goal for myself," said the ambitious investor. "I call it '50 by 50'—I want to own 50 single-family homes by the time I'm 50 years old. I'm on pace to achieve this milestone ahead of schedule and may need to set up a new goal for myself."

Michael has diversified his investing by purchasing single-family homes in six metropolitan areas: Oklahoma City, Oklahoma, three communities in Florida (Tampa, Orlando, Jacksonville), Atlanta, Georgia and Houston, Texas.

I asked Michael how he feels about his investing experiences, net worth, and his financial future.

> Michael answered as follows: "Buying rental homes has allowed me to build my own wealth and financial independence. I've become less dependent on corporate forces. I'm very happy that I did this. Real estate investing is like a part-time job for me now. I've continued to work in my industry too, but I'm no longer *solely* dependent on a job for my income and my quality of life."

When I say that buying additional homes in the future should almost be boring, this is what I mean. Like Michael, you too could become comfortable with the processes I've described to you so far. You too can buy whatever number of rental homes you need for your own financial plan. Remember that it all started the same way. Michael had to take his first steps to break the ice and complete basic training—just like you will do.

> Michael offers this advice to anyone who is still thinking about buying: "Jump in. Try it out. I recommend that if you go for it, you should have a longer horizon to own four or five rental homes at least. Why? When you own one home, it's a binary experience— the home is either rented and producing income for you (it's on) or it's not (it's off). As my portfolio of rental homes has grown,

the overall risk has been reduced. For example, if you have one vacancy and you own five homes, the income from the other four homes is making up for the month or two of vacancy that you might experience at some point. Also, when you have multiple properties under property management, it feels smoother. So, begin your investing with an internal commitment to buy several rental homes. You'll be glad you did."

REPLAY

- Title companies are neutral third parties that close real estate transactions and provide title insurance to buyers.

- "Basic training" is what I call the period from the moment your very first rental home closes and becomes yours until the home is rented.

- When basic training is over, and your home is rented, the time commitment to deposit rent checks and manage your property is typically 30 to 60 minutes each month.

- Save time. Let the professionals manage your single family home rental from the very beginning.

- As Michael's story demonstrates, buying home number one requires going through "basic training." After that, buying home number two is a repetition of the purchase of the first home; buying homes three, four, five—or 50—can eventually get repetitive, even "boring."

CHAPTER 8

How Nurses, Kindergarten Teachers, Firefighters, Massage Therapists, Engineers, Lawyers, Doctors and Foreigners Who Barely Speak English Can Retire Securely by Owning Single-Family Homes

I've noticed something disconcerting in my three decades as both an investor in single-family homes and as someone who's helped thousands of people build their future financial security. There's a misconception floating around out there that only professionals with degrees and large paychecks can—or should—become investors in real estate.

I am here to tell you 100%, without a doubt...this is absolutely not true.

Life doesn't really discriminate; it has a way of surprising anyone—at any time, so it is best for everyone to be prepared. That is what this chapter is about.

Sure, you've seen examples of engineers, lawyers, and doctors who have purchased single-family home rentals throughout this book. This chapter is instead *dedicated* to everyone. I hope it can be the spark to ignite a powerful wave of change. This chapter will show you how nurses, teachers, firefighters, designers, and others have successfully purchased single-family homes to secure themselves comfortable retirements.

You'll see several stories of ICG investors who just happen to be women. Because history and data show that women tend to outlive men, I believe women also should become investors in properties that can provide for them in the future. I have included the stories of women who decided to invest in single-family homes, letting those investors describe the difference it made in their lives years later after making that decision. I hope everyone will learn from these stories describing *why* people decide they *must* buy single-family homes. You'll see that life's circumstances and surprises can truly happen to anyone. It's best to be prepared.

The graphic designer's story

In early 2018, Dawn visited the ICG page on Facebook and wrote a nice post about her experience buying homes with us. This prompted me to want to learn more about her story. I found it powerful enough to include here.

Like so many, Dawn and her husband's only investment in real estate was buying their primary residence. They lived on Long Island and Dawn commuted to New York City for her career in graphic design. Everything was fine until quite suddenly she began experiencing back pain and surgeries, which lasted several years.

"In the middle of 2003, I began reconsidering my job, my future, and my ability to work," shared Dawn.

Like many women working full-time, Dawn said she frequently thought about activities to generate additional income.

"One day in 2003, I heard about the Learning Annex Education Company in NYC," Dawn recalls. "I went to a night class after work and met Adiel, the instructor. He made it sound so easy to buy single-family homes to make residual income. It was the first time I had ever attended a meeting to learn about investing in real estate. I was both very excited and nervous."

Dawn discussed what she learned with her husband, who was easily convinced to buy rental properties.

"It's been 15 years and I still remember what Adiel said," Dawn reflects. "He said, 'buy one property and you'll thank me later. Buy two single-family homes and in five years, you'll be one happy person.'"

At the end of 2003, Dawn and her husband took out a home equity loan.

"We decided to buy first in Keller, Texas," shares Dawn. "Lockheed Martin had just gotten a large government contract there. Adiel teaches investors to buy single-family homes only in places where there's growth and economic diversity. We flew out there and bought two properties in the same development—all new construction."

The following year, the couple moved to South Carolina. There, they bought and sold properties to generate cash to buy additional single-family homes.

"2007 wasn't a good time for me professionally as a graphic designer," shared Dawn. "We made the decision to move to Texas into one of our two properties. We lived in one home and enjoyed income from the second home. Even then, following Adiel's advice, we used a professional property manager to manage our rental in our own neighborhood."

By 2016, that second Texas home they had owned and rented for 13 years appreciated nicely.

"We had built up lots of equity, so we decided to sell it that year," Dawn recalls. "Before selling it, we called Adiel and asked where he and other ICG investors were buying."

That led Dawn to visit Oklahoma City and Jacksonville, Florida. The couple bought one single-family home in each of those two cities.

> "So, in effect, by selling one house we'd owned for 13 years, we were able to buy two homes in two cities. This has worked out nicely. Now we're almost 57 years old. We think we'll stay in Texas. We've doubled our monthly income now, with those two rental houses in Oklahoma City and Jacksonville providing us what we need."

Looking back and reflecting, she's got some advice for potential investors:

> "When we lived in South Carolina and owned two houses in Texas, we used that rental income to live on. If I could do it over again, I'd think twice about that. I would instead keep that income in a totally separate business account and build it up to buy more assets. The most single-family homes we ever owned at one time was four, while living in South Carolina. I wish we had purchased more."

Even so, Dawn feels very good about her current net worth and financial future.

> "Investing in single-family rental homes was the best decision my husband and I made, other than getting married," she said. "Knowing that we've done so well over the years, there's no stopping us now. As we get closer to retirement age, we'll buy more homes. As a matter of fact, in 2013, we bought and sold some other homes. We'll use that cash to buy more rental homes for the long term."

Here's the last piece of advice Dawn wants to give to people still thinking about buying:

> "In my life, I've always looked to better myself, to do better, learn more and do more. At age 42, we asked ourselves, 'what are we going to do for our retirement?' That open mindset, that

growth mindset I had is what led me to see that Learning Annex sign in NYC offering the chance to learn how to become an investor in single-family homes. I think it's important for people to understand they don't have to be homeowners to buy rental homes. Even if you're living in an apartment, you can still buy a home to rent out to others."

Dawn's story serves to remind *all* potential investors that your good health isn't guaranteed. If your ability to commute and work (to bring in the revenue you need to live on) is directly tied to good health… what will happen if your health suddenly changes? Do you have a plan in place?

If it isn't health taking a turn, what about the economy? As Dawn learned in 2007, industries and functional roles ebb and flow too. I fear for what they would have done if they did not buy those first homes only a few years earlier. Dawn's journey reminds us that (while I hope it will not be necessary) the rental homes you buy may one day save you from a financial crisis—one of these homes may even become your primary shelter if life changes drastically. While few investors entertain that possibility when buying, we should remember that life is unpredictable. She who owns several rental homes will most likely never be homeless.

And none of this would have happened without Dawn's open, growth-oriented mindset. She reminds potential investors to start the process with the intention of buying more than one building block for your financial future. Far from the exception, Dawn's words of, "I wish I had purchased more properties" are words I hear quite often. No matter who you are, or what your background, do not limit yourself when investing in your future.

The movie industry professional

Shifting gears, let's meet an ICG investor who was born outside the U.S. Nora lived in Los Angeles for 35 years and worked in the movie industry for most of that time. She's been buying and selling single-family homes for twenty years.

Nora began her story by saying, "I was a successful professional woman with a husband and two children. We owned two beautiful homes in Los Angeles. Most of the assets we accumulated came from my income working in the movie industry. I made good money. My husband was working much less, so he dedicated himself to taking care of our day-to-day operations. This included all of our financial dealings: paying bills, managing bank accounts, and the rest. I found it convenient for me to let him deal with all those details."

Like many busy women who are also mothers, Nora loved and enjoyed her work. She dedicated herself to it wholeheartedly. Then suddenly, life took a downward turn.

"When I was 40, I was diagnosed with cancer. This was totally unexpected and shattered my whole life. Everything came to a full stop."

It took two years for Nora to get back on her feet.

"I had lots of time to think things over and I decided to get a divorce. That was met with lots of resistance, of course. I ended up leaving my marriage with two kids and two suitcases."

That's when Nora learned the truth. The financial history *her* income had made possible was all in her ex-husband's name.

"I learned that all of our credit cards were in his name," she shared. "I was never listed as the primary card holder. When he had listed me, I was the secondary cardholder. Therefore, I had no credit history. It didn't matter to the credit companies that most of the charges on those cards were in my name. I was the one who traveled internationally, dined, and spent the money I earned. Yet, I was nobody for them."

As devastating as that was for her, Nora was determined to pick herself up and move forward. She quickly noticed many people were well-off financially because they had made real estate investments.

"I remembered a guy who worked for me, made less money than me, yet he was living a very nice life. He owned several homes that were doing well in the market. Through this colleague, I was introduced to Adiel after my recovery and divorce. I was 45 years old at the time."

In 1998, Nora called me and we arranged to meet in Northern California. She began to purchase single-family homes to provide for herself in the future. She eventually bought three single-family homes in Florida and Oklahoma. Nora emphasized that investing in single-family homes helped her financially over the years.

"These homes kept my money from losing value," she said. "Those three investments allowed me to keep my lifestyle in the short term. They also made me feel secure about the long term after my divorce."

Today Nora is a grandmother living comfortably overseas, retired after raising her two daughters. The three single-family homes she purchased in Florida and Oklahoma are providing her the extra income and security she needs in her sixties.

Nora's advice to people thinking about buying single-family rental homes is this: "When you decide to buy single-family homes, go with someone like Adiel. Before I started, I met others who had invested with his group. Those investors had only good things to say about him. Adiel is not only a total professional, he has also established a support base wherever he invests. Consequently, you feel like you're investing with him in these markets. There is already a tested mechanism to support your investing activities. In fact, I would only invest through Adiel's group because before he will recommend investing in a certain area, he will scout it out and research it thoroughly. He will establish his own industry relationships in the area. Most of all, he'll invest in homes there himself, hire property managers—everything. These actions make him a leader that's worth following."

The fireman and the nurse

Investing in single-family homes is not about the number of zeros on your paycheck. It's about how you prioritize and how much you set aside to invest.

Let me introduce you to Larry—one of several firefighters I know who have created portfolios of homes for their security. You'll see that with the right mindset and focused intent to create a solid financial future, busy working people of all types can indeed become investors.

Larry is a retired firefighter and ICG investor, who was first exposed to real estate investing by his fellow firefighters at the station. In their off-duty time, some firemen were buying homes to renovate and sell; others were buying single-family homes to rent and hold for the long term.

Larry said, "Firefighters love to be independent. We don't make tons of money as public-sector employees. We're usually looking for other ways to raise cash because we're not professionals with bigger salaries."

Larry was always looking ahead. "I wanted to buy real estate that would pay for my eventual child's education." You read that right. Even though he and his wife didn't yet have children, this firefighter was thinking about a future when he would be paying for a university education.

Larry began his investing career in 1989. His wife Lynn was a registered nurse. Her family-owned rental properties. He shared that Lynn was less afraid than he was about buying homes to rent.

I asked Larry how he raised capital to purchase his first single-family homes. His story is not only motivational but also instructive for anyone working in the public sector.

"We lived off my firefighter salary and used Lynn's salary to buy homes," Larry reveals.

He told me they both committed fully to investing for their future, even consciously choosing to turn their backs on consumer spending and limiting the number of times they would go out for dinner. They simply prioritized saving the nursing paycheck as investment capital. They didn't spend her paycheck on expensive vacations and other activities that many dual-income couples choose to spend on instead of investing.

Back then, Larry recalls, the popular rule about investing in real estate was to only buy within 30 miles of your own home and only for immediate positive cash flow.

"I had a friend who had attended several ICG Expos," Larry shared. "He suggested I go to Vegas to look at investment properties, and we did. Lynn and I ended up taking his place on a new house for which he had put down an earnest money deposit after he decided to buy elsewhere. My wife and I had not yet attended an Expo. At some point during the closing, I called Adiel. He invited my wife and me to come to an expo and learn about the infrastructure he was building for investors."

Larry and Lynn attended their first ICG Expo in 2001 in their mid-forties. They bought three more houses in Vegas utilizing the in-place ecosystem they connected with that day.

"We both liked his philosophy," shared Larry. "I liked buying and putting some money in my pocket. I liked having tenants pay so one day I'd own the property. The side benefit my wife and I enjoyed was we turned our investment activities into places to go on vacation together."

Some peers thought Larry was breaking the commonly-accepted rules about investing—buying and renting properties in Las Vegas, Nevada when he lived in San Jose, California.

"When I started investing over there, my older firefighting friends mocked me," he said. "But the younger ones came to Adiel's expos with me. Four other firefighters bought homes in Vegas to rent to families. Some of those firefighters later sold those homes to buy their primary residence in the San Francisco Bay Area. Some held on to them as income properties like I did."

At one point, the firefighter and the nurse owned 18 houses. Today they own 12 homes in three states, having sold the homes they bought in Arizona and Las Vegas.

I asked Larry how he feels about his successful investment journey after having connected with ICG.

"It's changed my life because I know that if I had done this on my own, I'd maybe own three or four houses in Bay Area," he posits. "I doubt my wife and I would be enjoying the cash flow we have now. I certainly wouldn't have the flexibility to move around as I do. I retired ten years ago at age 53. Now I have time to volunteer with the Association of Retired Firefighters in San Jose, something that's near and dear to my heart."

Larry has a philosophy that's worth appreciating and perhaps emulating.

"I see single-family home investing like saving in soda cans," he says. "I make a few pennies on each one initially and in time, it adds up very nicely. A lot of retirees have to get second jobs to stay here in the Bay Area. I don't have to work. If we didn't have my single-family homes generating income for us, we couldn't stay here."

Lastly, Larry shared that he just helped his daughter move into her first house. The real estate investing torch has been shared. The child the young firefighter once imagined before she was even born, the child for whom he knew he would need extra income to put through college, has just become a homeowner herself! I'd call the story of the firefighter and the nurse a success on multiple levels.

ECOSYSTEM BENEFIT
Tried and Tested Infrastructure Enabling Working
People to Invest and be Supported

"Adiel has all the connections you need in these markets. You
don't need to take a lot of time to search for real estate agents,
for insurance agents, or for property managers. Plus, we usually
get a discount off property management fees because we're
part of this large group. Since my husband and I are inclined
to purchase new homes as we've learned from Adiel, we can
do this easily through ICG. That way, the appliances are new,
so it usually takes years before you have to spend money to
repair or replace things. I don't have to worry about it. I only

need to look at the income going into my account. Since 2003, when we started working with Adiel, I can't tell you of a time I emailed him and didn't get a response. He responds and hooks you up to somebody who can help. Recently, we were looking at putting our properties into an LLC. Within a couple days, I got an answer from Adiel and a referral to exactly who I needed to make the transfer easy. We know we're working with people Adiel trusts, so I can trust them. It's been a pleasure."
—Dawn, an ICG investor for 15 years who began investing in her early forties and now owns three homes in Texas, Oklahoma, and Florida

REPLAY

- **People in a wide variety of professions have successfully purchased single-family homes to secure themselves comfortable retirements.**

- **It's not about how much money you receive in a paycheck that matters. It's about how you prioritize those funds and how much you keep to invest.**

- **The ICG infrastructure enables many types of working people to become investors in single-family homes and be supported.**

CHAPTER 9

I've Built the Infrastructure — Now It's Your Turn

Are you confident, after reading my tips and the words of investors who have put those tips to use, that now it's your turn to safeguard your financial future?

I hope so.

Remember the most important tip of all, advice you've seen several investors repeat: there's no need to do this alone. You can invest within an ecosystem that will hold your hand through the entire process of buying your single-family rental homes. We've already helped thousands of investors build their portfolios.

But I get it. You, like most people who want to build portfolios of single-family homes, are busy. You already have a career and a full life. I understand that you want to act. You know you *need* to take action, but very likely you've discovered one big problem...there's an entire industry out there making noise about real estate investing. They're saying you need to learn more before you start buying properties. Perhaps someone somewhere made you feel that you're not ready to buy yet. Maybe they made you feel you want to be perfectly ready before you buy rental homes.

Guess what? That is analysis paralysis. It's also why I wrote this book. I don't want you to succumb to this. You don't need to pay a bunch of experts thousands of dollars to teach you how to buy cheap, distressed properties. You don't need to pay for classes and boot camps. I say use your hard-earned cash not for boot camps but as *down payments* to buy quality single-family homes!

It's time to cut through all the noise.

Just focus on how I've done it. Learn these top tips you need to buy single-family homes. Absorb the advice I shared in this book, knowing thousands of investors have successfully followed it. It's time to stop over-analyzing and feeling like you'll never be ready. It's time to take action and decide to buy a rental home in the next six months (or so) because now you know you can invest with a proven ecosystem of professionals. You just need to decide to take the first step to start.

I've seen another version of analysis paralysis, one that's especially true for those meeting regularly with financial planners. Many of these professionals advise you to purchase stocks and bonds for your retirement (quite simply because that's what they've been trained to do). Many of them have no training whatsoever on the economics and inflation-beating advantages of real estate properties such as you've learned in this book, so naturally they recommend securities. That's why it's important for *you* to understand the advantages of single-family homes that thousands of investors are enjoying now.

We addressed investing in stocks earlier in this book. I stated that they are a fine investment and should most certainly be one of the pillars of your financial planning. But you shouldn't limit your retirement assets to those securities. The same goes for bonds.

Stocks and bonds cannot be bought with a small down payment and an amazing 30-year fixed-rate loan. This advantage only exists for houses. It's true that some stocks may also pay dividends, but no stock has little tenants living in it and paying ever-higher rents since they need a place to live.

Even the iconic investor Warren Buffett, who is not typically known as an investor in homes, wanted to buy single-family rentals in large quantities in the aftermath of the recession in 2012. He and I communicated back and forth on this topic and he told me how he would prefer to buy houses (since he has plenty of cash on hand and every option available to him). As the brilliant man he is, he wanted to buy thousands of homes for his company, Berkshire Hathaway, using a 20% down payment and a 30-year fixed-rate loan on each and every house. Amazingly, the rules of FNMA limited even him to a mere ten loans of this type. Needless to say, he could've gotten different types of loans, like commercial loans, for all the homes he planned on buying, but he wanted the magical 30-year fixed-rate loan because he understands its power over the long term.

So, yes, quality single-family home rentals have the power to completely change and vastly improve your financial future. They should at least be one of the pillars of your retirement security. Don't let anyone talk you out of investing in single-family homes simply because they don't understand what you do.

Overcome the fear

I've addressed the common fears I hear from people, like "What if I buy a home and it doesn't rent?". I've shown you that working within an infrastructure minimizes you becoming overcome by fear. You've seen by now how the ICG ecosystem of professionals works to help people find, evaluate, and purchase single-family homes. Assuming you've already identified the source of your down payment and know you'll qualify for the financing through a 30-year fixed-rate loan (either on your own, with your spouse, or with a partner or family member) there really is no reason not to start taking action right now to buy a single-family home in the next six months. The only delay that may surface could be one caused by your own fear.

I recommend that whatever scares you most, go back through this book and read my advice for overcoming that fear. Reread an investor success story to understand how the thing you fear was resolved. Then realize that you, working within our infrastructure, *can* do this.

There is no reason to delay

I've been doing this for well over 30 years. I've seen the lives of thousands of people change as a result of this activity. This doesn't happen in one year—I've articulated that we're working with a long-term span: 10, 15, maybe 20 years. In time, rents will go higher as the amount you owe on your loan goes lower and inflation erodes your 30-year fixed-rate loan—it's a sweet situation.

When I meet with some investors today, they tell me proudly of the eight (or so) homes they own. They tell me how those properties became the cornerstone of their retirement. Others talk about the 16 homes they own and how they're happy they don't have to work anymore. Don't you want to join this group of people who created a portfolio of single-family homes providing their income and increasing their net worth?

As I hear those stories from investors, there's typically one sentence they say: "I wish I had bought more houses."

Even I, after nearly 35 years, having purchased more homes than any ICG investor, think it: *I should have bought more properties.*

So today is a great day to begin buying single-family homes. Right now, interest rates are extremely low. When I began investing, interest rates were about 14%. I remember the happy day when rates went down to a *single digit,* and everyone happily refinanced to the rate of 9.95%. Historically, a 7.5% rate was considered very low. At the time of this publication, rates are even lower than that! Investors can get rates slightly over 3.3% fixed for 30 years! (Remember that investor rates are a bit higher than homeowners' rates).

Please don't let interest rates creeping up .25% every once in a while keep you from buying the assets that can totally transform your future. Feel free to repeat this sentence to yourself, "Adiel began buying when rates were 14%. I can do this!" So, decide to do it and fix the current low rate forever. Let these low interest rates turbocharge your investment portfolio.

Nike® has it right—JUST DO IT®

We will support you any way we can.

So, if you want to rest, you have to invest. Don't wait. Let me help you get started. This is very doable and a lot simpler than you think. This will create financial strength and income for your future, even if your future is very long.

It is so exciting to me that you can change your future dramatically with what you've learned in this book. I can't wait to help you and hold your hand in making this change!

ECOSYSTEM BENEFIT
We're Ready to Help You Right Now

We're ready now to help you start the process of buying your single-family home. The infrastructure is in place. Maybe you already own single-family home rentals and are ready to buy in different markets where we invest. We will start where you are—whether you're buying your first home or adding to your portfolio of rental homes.

Here's what one investor whom you met earlier (Michael), said about the advantages of working with our ecosystem as you grow your portfolio:

> "I reached out to Adiel when I wanted to diversify into more markets. I was buying a lot of homes in Oklahoma and didn't want to be too concentrated in one place. I called to hear about his experiences about buying in different cities. I wanted to buy in Atlanta, Georgia. He connected me with someone he knows there, who was very helpful to me. Adiel has a sizable, quality network that he shares with investors as we grow our portfolios."

So, you see, we'll be with you as you take this journey toward building your potentially amazing financial future. You won't feel alone. Even when you've mastered the process...after you've purchased your 4th, 5th, 6th rental home...you won't be alone (unless you want to be) because by then, you might be thinking of selling one nicely appreciating property to buy two other homes in different cities. (Note: Many ICG investors will commonly use a tax-deferred 1031 Exchange to do this. I cover the process in detail in *Remote Control Retirement Riches* if you're curious, but I will not get into the details here.) Rest assured—when the time comes for you to sell a property and you need that guidance, I'll hold your hand through that too.

After you read the last page of this book, please take the first step to start buying your single-family home rental. Simply send us an email with your phone number at info@icgre.com. Our staff will call you to set up a phone meeting, quite possibly directly with me.

If you wish to call instead, please call us at (800) 324-3983. If you're calling from outside the U.S., call us in the San Francisco Bay Area at (415) 927-7504.

Now, if you find yourself extra motivated to take the next step and see the variety of single-family home rentals available now to our investors, please visit icgre.com. There you can join our "Quick Send List" and receive the information existing ICG investors receive about events and markets. While at our site, you can see the schedule of our quarterly ICG Expo events.

Hopefully, you will plan to join us in person soon. People fly in from around the country to attend our Expo, usually held next to the San Francisco airport. There, you'll meet the teams from various markets who present key demographic and economic information about their markets to all in attendance. They'll show you the homes they have available for you to purchase at that moment. You'll learn about important issues such as buying single-family homes within a self-directed IRA, asset preservation & protection, tax issues for investors, the mechanics of 1031 tax-deferred exchanges, overall financial planning, and many other subjects of value. We bring experts in these fields to teach us at these events. You'll meet mortgage brokers licensed to initiate investor loans in all fifty states. You will listen to and can participate in extensive and deep Q&A sessions, plus hear a lot of information from yours truly. You'll meet investors who have been investing with ICG's infrastructure for years. It's all there. All you need to do is decide to join us for the day.

As of the writing of this book, in Q3 of 2021, our events are held online via Zoom. While I like the live event and enjoy meeting you and other investors, there is an element of ease for an online event, as people can join from anywhere in the world with no need to travel.

I can't wait to hear from you, and I look forward to meeting you soon!

QUARTERLY EXPOS

There's an admission fee to attend, but *simply by mentioning this book when you email or call us,* you can attend for free. Just email us at info@icgre.com and tell us which Expo you want to attend. If you wish to bring a guest, please provide your guest's name, so our staff can add them to the free attendance list. We have now made the process even easier: You can register directly on our website, at no cost, for our online events. Your friends can also register. Just go to our website: icgre.com and register under EVENTS.

INVESTOR STORY
In His Own Words

Like many kids who grew up in military families, Phil moved around —a *lot.*

> "I grew up as an Army brat; we lived all over the world. I lived in Japan, Italy, and Australia before I even went to high school. Until my father retired from the Army, we never had a real 'home'."

Phil followed in his father's Army footsteps. While serving in Washington D.C. as a captain, he first dipped his toe into investing in real estate on the East Coast.

> "I met a senior Army officer whose wife was in the real estate business. She told me that for what I was paying for my apartment, I could use my military benefits and buy my own home. She walked me through my first purchase, a one-bedroom, one bath Colonial-style house in Arlington, Virginia. I bought it for $24,000 in 1971 at the age of 25. Four years later, I sold it for $36,000."

On his next assignment, while stationed in San Francisco, Phil invested again in 1975.

> "My second house was a three-bedroom, two-bath home in Larkspur, California. I paid $36,000 for it. I sold it four years later in 1979 for $75,000 and thought I was a real estate genius. I sold it because by then I had left the Army, completed graduate school at Stanford and was moving back to the East Coast to take a job in the investment banking world. I never thought I'd return to California. That same house in Larkspur was on the market, renovated, just last year for $2 million. Some genius, right?"

When asked what made Phil begin buying and holding onto single-family homes, he shared this two-part answer:

> "I think of single-family homes as full of memories: family celebrations, holidays, pictures pulled out of albums in later years of children at Christmas, or in Halloween costumes, dogs and cats and hamsters. For me, having moved so often in childhood, the term 'home' means a lot. My thoughts about single-family homes are of permanence—warm, sheltering places. These homes are ideal for renting to families to make these memories. Secondly, I like single-family homes because each one is different, and my investment returns have been so much better than the stock market."

Phil and his wife Lisa connected with us in 2004, introduced by mutual friends in Marin County who were ICG investors. He commented on what it's been like for them since that first meeting.

> Phil said, "My previous experiences investing in single-family homes on both coasts, plus Adiel's guidance and approach, led us to want to buy more homes. We saw that he does very thorough diligence on the areas he suggests for investment; he has created a 'turnkey' situation for investors. He's done the demographics and economic assessment on the cities and

areas he recommends. He has carefully vetted brokers and
property managers to assist investors. So, we bought three
single-family homes in 2005 and 2006: one in Austin, Texas,
and two in a suburb of Phoenix, Arizona. We bought all three
using Adiel's brokers in those cities—Tom in Austin and Jim
in Phoenix. They were highly professional. All three homes
were under management by local property managers who have
always been responsive to questions on market conditions and
sale situations."

Phil shared that over the years, all three homes appreciated
significantly, although there were several years when there was
slower growth. Lisa and Phil sold one of the homes in Austin and
are continuing to buy.

I met Phil and Lisa 14 years ago. Like so many ICG investors, we
sometimes go years without chatting. But when they've needed advice
and guidance, we've been there for them. Phil recalls a recent example.

"Recently, after re-financing two of our rental houses, I called Adiel after not having done so for almost ten years. It was as if we'd last talked just last week. He gave me a thorough overview of the Oklahoma City market, and he followed up immediately with introductions by email to his mortgage broker and to Joe, his recommended real estate broker in Oklahoma City. Consequently, we're about to buy a single-family home in a good suburb there, which will bring our total to three rental homes... for now," said Phil.

Asked how he and Lisa feel today about the portfolio they've built, Phil answered this way:

"I think investing in single-family homes was one of the wisest things we could've done. I am glad we did so. We're very happy with our net worth, our credit rating, and our financial future. For us, the equity is paramount, even if the income may be marginally positive. The investments really can carry themselves. We can refinance them or sell them later. We're using one property to finance our daughter's university education. All our homes are in our family trust."

I asked Phil what advice he would give to someone who's still thinking about buying.

"The markets don't wait," said Phil. "We're at a historically low spot with interest rates. Adiel's recommendations are worth taking seriously—for all the reasons he cites. Particularly worth noting is the 30-year fixed-rate loans available in the U.S., which enables the mortgages to be paid off by your tenants in your rental homes, without the loans ever being adjusted for inflation. I appreciate his thorough research and diligence. When you decide to buy, I would strongly advise visiting the cities and areas where you're considering investing. However, given the wealth of information available via the Internet, coupled with Adiel's advice and in-place support structure, it's currently possible to invest without physically doing so. It's a personal choice."

The man who grew up as a military brat moving frequently is truly at *home*. He and Lisa are back in California, the state where he once thought he'd never return. Having learned the San Francisco Bay Area lesson of Larkspur decades ago (when he sold that house for $75,000 and felt like a genius), this time around in 1993, he and Lisa bought their permanent four-bedroom rancher home in Marin County for $390,000 and held on. You can only imagine how happy they are with that decision.

REPLAY

- Do not succumb to analysis paralysis.
- Overcome your fears by rereading the words of actual investors and the tips in this book.
- There is no reason not to start soon.
- Think like Nike®—JUST DO IT® We will support you any way we can.
- If you want to rest in the future, it would be wise to invest.

Email or call us to get started soon.
info@icgre.com
(800) 324-3983 or (415) 927-7504

GLOSSARY

Adjustable Rate Loan (ARM)
A loan with a variable interest rate that rises or falls according to the index to which it is tied.

Adjusted Gross Income
Your taxable income after deductions.

Annual Percentage Rate (APR)
This reflects the true annual cost of a loan. The APR is determined by adding the interest rate to the loan fees and is expressed as a percentage.

Appraisal
An estimate of property value produced by an independent appraiser.

Appreciation
The increase of property value.

Capital Gains
The taxable profits derived from the sale or exchange of a capital asset, such as real property.

Cash Flow
The difference between expenses and income. For example, if a property has an income of $10,000 and expenses of $4000, it has a $6000 positive cash flow. If expenses are $12,000, it has a $2000 negative cash flow.

Closing
Also known as Settlement. Closing is the act of finalizing all arrangements between the buyer and seller. Money is disbursed, the deed is prepared in the new owner's name, and the property is conveyed in accordance with the contract signed by both parties.

Closing Costs
The fees associated with the closing of escrow, or of a loan.

Coronavirus
Coronaviruses are a type of virus. There are many different kinds, and some cause disease. A newly identified coronavirus, SARS-CoV-2, has caused a worldwide pandemic of respiratory illness, called COVID-19.

COVID-19
COVID-19 an infectious disease caused by a coronavirus discovered in 2019/2020.

Depreciation
Loss against the property (for tax purposes only), prorated over 27.5 years for residential property.

Equity
The cash value of a property, less any outstanding mortgages and liens.

Escrow
A trust account wherein deposit money is held by a neutral third party (usually an escrow officer or title company) prior to finalization of the sale. When escrow is "closed," it means the transaction has been completed: the seller is paid, and the buyer takes title to the property.

Fixed-Rate Loan
A loan with an interest rate that does not change over the life of the loan.

Flip
To sell a property soon after buying it (ideally for a quick profit.)

Foreclosure
When a property owner defaults on the mortgage and the lender takes possession of the property.

Hybrid Loan
A loan which combines an Adjustable Rate Loan (ARM) and Fixed-Rate Loan.

Improvement Value
The cost of the property less the cost of the land. When you take a depreciation deduction, you may only take depreciation against the cost of the structure, not the land. The structure is also known as the "improvements."

Interest
What lenders charge for the use of their money. Interest is expressed as a percentage, or interest rate, which is a factor of the APR.

Leverage
To borrow and use other people's money, generally a bank's or lending institution's.

Lien
A claim against property, which can include mortgages, trusts, and unpaid property taxes. The primary purpose of a title search is to be certain all liens are known at the day of settlement.

Market
An area, usually defined by city, in which to invest.

Median Price
Median means "in the middle." So, with regard to List Price, this means exactly half of homes listed are above this price and exactly half are below. For example, let's say there are 5 homes for sale in a market at prices of $175,000, $200,000, $250,000,

$350,000, and $600,000. The median price would be the one in the middle, or $250,000.

Net Worth
The wealth you've accumulated to date (i.e., what's left after subtracting your liabilities from your assets).

No Money Down
Can also be thought of as 100% financing. If you borrow money for the down payment, then you have purchased a property with 100% financing, or no money down.

Pandemic
A disease prevalent over a whole country or the world.

Pass Through Deduction
The Tax Cuts and Jobs Act (HR 1, "TCJA") established a new tax deduction for owners of pass-through businesses. Pass-through owners who qualify can deduct up to 20% of their net business income from their income taxes, reducing their effective income tax rate by 20%. This deduction began in 2018 and is scheduled to last through 2025—that is, it will end on January 1, 2026, unless extended by Congress.

Points
An up-front fee paid to the lender at closing. One point equals 1% of the loan amount (i.e., one point of a $100,000 loan would be $1000).

Principal
The loan amount, which is paid off in part each month, along with the interest payment.

Private Mortgage Insurance (PMI)
When you make a down payment of less than 20%, lenders require you carry private mortgage insurance, or PMI. PMI protects lenders from financial loss if the homeowner goes into Foreclosure.

Profit & Loss Statement
An accounting of your investment's income and expenses, which will show either profit or loss.

Property Manager
For a fee (generally between 8% and 10% of the gross rent collected) a property manager can handle all aspects of renting and maintaining your investment property, from leasing to repairs.

Refinance
To secure new financing for a property, whether by securing a new first mortgage, an equity loan, or a second mortgage.

Repair
Repairs are fully deductible expenses for items and services that keep the property operational. These are sometimes confused with Capital Improvements, which are different (see definition).

Retirement Account
A long-term savings and investment account. Popular retirement accounts include IRAs, 401(k)s and Keogh plans.

Return
The amount of profit realized from an investment. For example, if you make $4000 on a $10,000 investment, that's a 40% return.

Settlement
See Closing.

Single-Family Home
A single-family home is a single unit, detached dwelling with a yard.

ABOUT THE AUTHOR

Adiel Gorel has more than three decades of successful real estate investing experience. As the CEO of ICG (International Capital Group) Real Estate, a world-renowned real estate investment firm founded in the San Francisco Bay Area in 1987, Adiel has helped investors utilize one of the most powerful investment tools—real estate. He teaches people how to have fun with a process most find complex and speaks about the importance of securing a strong financial future for retirement, business investing, and college education.

He is also the author of *Remote Control Retirement Riches: How to Change Your Future with Rental Homes*, which includes plans and examples of how investors can achieve powerful financial futures.

For over 30 years, ICG has hosted a 1-Day Expo each quarter, bringing expert speakers, market teams from all over the country, and hundreds of investors to the San Francisco Bay Area. During the COVID pandemic, these events are held via Zoom. ICG has an infrastructure of teams nationwide, supporting their investors

Adiel has been featured on NBC, ABC, in *Fortune Magazine*, the *San Francisco Examiner*, and numerous radio shows showcasing his no-nonsense, insightful approach to real estate investing. He was invited to create a Public Television program called "Remote Control Retirement Riches," and later a public television program on health and wellness called "Life 201." *The Adiel Gorel Show*, his podcast on health and wellness, is featured on many online media outlets such as YouTube, Spotify, Apple Music, and others.

Adiel also creates music. He writes, sings, and plays lead guitar on original songs, which are also featured on the above online media outlets. He speaks worldwide and throughout the U.S., sharing his knowledge on a variety of topics, including securing a powerful financial future, investing in single-family homes, the 30-year fixed-rate mortgage, and related subjects.

ICG has established an infrastructure to support investors in many metropolitan areas in the U.S. Gorel owns many properties himself.

To this day, Adiel supports individual investors via planning, assistance in remote home buying, and property management issues resolution.

He holds a master's degree from Stanford University. His professional experience includes being a Hewlett-Packard research engineer, as well as management and director positions at Excel Telecommunications and several biotechnology firms. He lives in the San Francisco Bay Area.

INDEX

Made in the USA
Las Vegas, NV
18 August 2023

76291467R00105